ROMEO AND JULIET
GCSE REVISION WORKBOOK

HELEN BACKHOUSE

OXFORD
UNIVERSITY PRESS

Contents

OXFORD
UNIVERSITY PRESS

Great Clarendon Street, Oxford, OX2 6DP, United Kingdom

Oxford University Press is a department of the University of Oxford.

It furthers the University's objective of excellence in research, scholarship, and education by publishing worldwide. Oxford is a registered trade mark of Oxford University Press in the UK and in certain other countries

© Oxford University Press 2022

The moral rights of the author have been asserted

First published in 2022

All rights reserved. No part of this publication may be reproduced, stored in a retrieval system, or transmitted, in any form or by any means, without the prior permission in writing of Oxford University Press, or as expressly permitted by law, by licence or under terms agreed with the appropriate reprographics rights organization. Enquiries concerning reproduction outside the scope of the above should be sent to the Rights Department, Oxford University Press, at the address above.

You must not circulate this work in any other form and you must impose this same condition on any acquirer

British Library Cataloguing in Publication Data
Data available

978-1-38-203242-1

10 9 8 7 6 5 4 3 2 1

Paper used in the production of this book is a natural, recyclable product made from wood grown in sustainable forests.

The manufacturing process conforms to the environmental regulations of the country of origin.

Printed in Great Britain by Bell and Bain Ltd., Glasgow

Acknowledgements
The publisher would like to thank the following for permissions to use copyright material:

Cover: Silke Bachmann

Artwork: Aptara

Photos: p6: Donald Cooper/Alamy Stock Photo; **p16:** AF archive/Alamy Stock Photo; **p26:** Donald Cooper/Alamy Stock Photo; **p36:** robbie jack/Corbis via Getty Images; **p46:** robbie jack/Corbis via Getty Images; **p56:** Donald Cooper/Alamy Stock Photo; **p64:** Donald Cooper/Alamy Stock Photo; **p72:** Donald Cooper/Alamy Stock Photo; **p80:** Tony Kyriacou/Shutterstock; **p88:** © Photostage.co.uk;

Although we have made every effort to trace and contact all copyright holders before publication this has not been possible in all cases. If notified, the publisher will rectify any errors or omissions at the earliest opportunity.

Introduction

There are two things you need to succeed in any literature exam:

1. knowledge of the text
2. the skill to be able to write about it.

This book focuses on these two things by developing your knowledge of characters and themes, and then helping you develop your essay-writing skills. You should:

- make sure you know the basic plot and structure of the play

- attempt all the tasks in each unit

- follow the advice below about writing responses.

Five tips for writing responses

Essay-style responses test several skills. Here are some tips about what makes a good response:

1. Question focus is vital – this means making sure you are staying focused on the task you are given. Identify the key words in the task and make sure that every paragraph you write is relevant to the question.

2. Including references to support your points is important. Sometimes direct quotation is used but there is no link between the number and extent of quotations you use and your final mark. Referring to events is fine but remember you can only do this if you know the play well.

3. Good responses have a direction. From the start they argue a viewpoint and explain it clearly throughout the essay. Practise writing opening paragraphs that clearly set out your overall view on the task.

4. You will need to comment on the playwright's methods – how the play is structured and how the language is used. Remember that structure means:
   - how characters develop and change during the play

   - where key events are placed in the storyline

   - how conflicts and problems develop and how they are resolved at the end

   - the level of knowledge given to the audience and characters – who knows what and when.

5. Don't 'force' context into your response. The tasks you are given naturally invite you to write about the play in the context of universal themes such as power, love and mortality. Modern literature courses often view contexts, ideas and themes as overlapping concepts. In this book, the phrase 'contexts/ideas' is used to signify this. Be careful if you choose to include historical context – often, it doesn't help to answer the tasks set.

Plot summary

In *Romeo and Juliet*, the story of two 'star crossed lovers' who fall in love despite their families being enemies, Shakespeare explores themes of love, conflict, youth, power and freedom in a play which has been loved by audiences for hundreds of years.

★ Key turning points in the play

Act 1

- A street fight between the Capulets and the Montagues takes place.

★ The Prince forbids further fighting, on pain of death.

- Romeo is unhappily in love with Rosaline, who refuses his love.

- Lord Capulet arranges a marriage for his daughter to Paris.

- Juliet is naïve and obedient in following her parents' wishes.

★ Romeo meets and falls in love with Juliet at the Capulet ball.

Act 2

- Romeo meets Juliet secretly on her balcony and they promise to marry.

- The Friar agrees to marry the young couple the following day.

- Romeo keeps his new love a secret from his friends Mercutio and Benvolio.

- The Nurse helps Romeo and Juliet secretly arrange the wedding.

★ In secret, against their families' wishes, Romeo and Juliet are married.

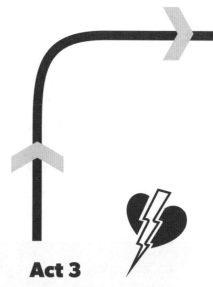

Act 3

★ Tybalt challenges Romeo to a fight but Mercutio takes the challenge and is killed.

★ Romeo kills Tybalt to avenge Mercutio's death and is exiled by the Prince.

- Juliet is devastated by the news and agonises with the Nurse what to do.

- The Friar advises Romeo to visit Juliet and flee Verona in the morning.

★ The Capulets, sad about Tybalt's death, force Juliet to marry Paris.

- Juliet refuses to marry Paris and her parents threaten to disown her.

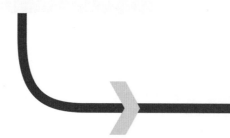

Act 4

- Juliet seeks help from the Friar, her only remaining friend.

- The Friar devises an ambitious plan to help Juliet avoid marrying Paris.

- Juliet, as instructed, apologises to her parents and agrees to marry Paris.

★ Juliet, on the advice of the Friar, takes a sleeping potion to avoid marrying Paris.

- The Capulets are devastated by Juliet's 'death' and arrange her funeral.

Act 5

- Romeo hears the news of Juliet's 'death' and vows to return to die by her side.

- The Friar realises his plan has failed as important letters have not been sent.

- Paris encounters Romeo at the tomb, they fight, and Paris is killed.

★ Romeo lies beside Juliet's body, drinks poison and dies, just as Juliet wakes.

★ The Friar tries to escape with Juliet, but she sees Romeo and kills herself.

★ The Prince declares all are punished as the Montagues and Capulets make peace.

Character list

Prince Escales – Prince of Verona

Mercutio – his kinsman, Romeo's friend

Paris – another kinsman, suitor to Juliet

Lord Montague – head of a noble family in Verona; the Montague family have been enemies with the Capulet family for a long time

Lady Montague – his wife

Romeo – his son

Benvolio – his nephew, Romeo's friend

Abram – servant of Lord Montague

Balthasar – servant of Lord Montague

Lord Capulet – head of a noble family in Verona which is hostile to the Montagues

Lady Capulet – his wife

Juliet – his daughter

Cousin Capulet – his relative

Tybalt – Lady Capulet's nephew

Nurse – to Juliet

Peter – servant of Lord Capulet

Sampson – servant of Lord Capulet

Gregory – servant of Lord Capulet

Friar Lawrence – a Franciscan friar

Friar John – a Franciscan friar

An Apothecary

The Chorus

Romeo

Key ideas about Romeo

1. Romeo is the **tragic hero** of the play.
2. He is the son of one of the leading families in Verona, the Montagues. How Romeo deals with the bonds of family and friendship helps drive the action of the story.
3. His relationship with Juliet is the central element of the play and the name 'Romeo' has become a **symbol** of romantic love.
4. He sees himself as a victim of fate, with his life influenced by chance meetings and events.
5. As a man, Romeo is presented in different guises: a passionate lover, a loyal friend, and a vengeful fighter.

Key quotations

'fire-ey'd fury be my conduct now!' (Romeo, Act 3 Scene 1)

'O, I am fortune's fool.' (Romeo, Act 3 Scene 1)

Romeo believes himself to be a puppet whose strings are pulled by supernatural forces beyond his control. Here, Shakespeare uses **alliteration** to emphasise Romeo's feeling that he is being mocked.

'Thus with a kiss I die.' (Romeo, Act 5 Scene 3)

'Did my heart love till now?' (Romeo, Act 1 Scene 5)

Key events and structure

Act 1 Scene 1
Romeo tells Benvolio his love for Rosaline has been rejected.

Act 1 Scene 5
Romeo attends the Capulet party in disguise and falls in love with Juliet, the host's daughter, at first sight.

Act 2 Scene 2
Romeo meets Juliet on her balcony the same night and promises to marry her.

Act 2 Scene 6
Supported by the Friar, Romeo secretly marries Juliet.

Act 3 Scene 1
Romeo encounters Tybalt, who kills Mercutio and is in turn killed by Romeo, who is then exiled.

Act 3 Scene 5
Advised by the Friar, Romeo spends one night with Juliet, then flees the city.

Act 5 Scene 1
Romeo, in despair after hearing about Juliet's 'death', buys poison to end his life.

Act 5 Scene 3
Romeo kills Paris, then lies beside Juliet in the Capulet tomb, takes the poison and dies.

Exploring Romeo
First impressions in Act 1 Scene 1

Activity 1

Romeo's parents, Lord and Lady Montague, and Benvolio discuss Romeo before the audience sees him for the first time. When Romeo arrives, he tells Benvolio about his **unrequited love** for Rosaline.

a. Circle the words you think best describe Romeo in this scene.

passionate	sullen	lonely	volatile	immature
despairing	dejected	loyal	melancholy	stubborn

b. Describe your first impression of Romeo using at least three words from the box above.

----

c. Why do you think Shakespeare decided not to include Rosaline in the play, except by name?

Romeo meets Juliet in Act 1 Scene 5

Activity 2

Read the following speech that Romeo makes when he catches sight of Juliet for the first time in Act 1 Scene 5. Match each statement on the right to the quotation that illustrates it. The first one has been done for you.

O she doth teach the torches to burn bright!
It seems she hangs upon the cheek of night
As a rich jewel in an Ethiop's ear—
Beauty too rich for use, for earth too dear:
So shows a snowy dove trooping with crows,
As yonder lady o'er her fellows shows.
The measure done, I'll watch her place of stand,
And touching hers, make blessed my rude hand.
Did my heart love till now? forswear it, sight!
For I ne'er saw true beauty till this night.

He is intent on watching her.

He thinks Juliet stands out from the crowd.

He finds Juliet beautiful.

He thinks Juliet appears pure and innocent.

He has forgotten about Rosaline.

He has had a sudden change of heart.

Romeo and the language of love

Activity 3

Shakespeare's writing is full of dramatic **imagery**. The images are often extended throughout the play to become **motifs**, such as light and stars, which can link to the themes of the play.

a. Read the speech that Romeo makes when Juliet appears on her balcony in Act 2 Scene 2. Using one colour, highlight any words, phrases or imagery that relate to light and darkness. Then, using another colour, highlight those that relate to heaven and the skies.

> Two of the fairest stars in all the heaven,
>
> Having some business, do entreat her eyes,
>
> To twinkle in their spheres till they return.
>
> What if her eyes were there, they in her head?
>
> The brightness of her cheek would shame those stars,
>
> As daylight doth a lamp; her eyes in heaven
>
> Would through the airy region stream so bright
>
> That birds would sing and think it were not night.

b. Explain how Shakespeare uses motifs of light and darkness or heaven and the skies to convey Romeo's feelings. Remember to analyse the language used in the quotations you have identified.

----

c. The speech is a **soliloquy**, so only the audience hears Romeo's words. What effect does this create for the audience?

Tip

Making references and comparisons to other parts of the play can be useful to demonstrate a deeper knowledge. For example, you could refer back to how Romeo describes his love for Rosaline in Act 1 Scene 1, when he tells Benvolio **'Love is a smoke made with the fume of sighs'**, as if love is an invisible and cruel force, causing only misery and despair.

Romeo's relationships

Romeo appears in almost every Act of the play, and many of his scenes are with just one other character. This allows the audience to see different dimensions to Romeo's character.

a. Explain what the following quotations suggest about the relationship between Romeo and Friar Lawrence. The first one has been done for you.

Quotation	What it shows about Romeo's relationship
'Hence will I to my ghostly sire's close cell, His help to crave, and my dear hap to tell.' (Romeo, Act 2 Scene 2)	Romeo chooses to tell the Friar of his new love and ask for his help rather than his parents'.
'I'll tell thee as we pass, but this I pray, That thou consent to marry us today.' (Romeo, Act 2 Scene 3)	
'But come, young waverer, come go with me, In one respect I'll thy assistant be' (Friar Lawrence, Act 2 Scene 3)	

b. In the space below, make a spidergram exploring Romeo's relationships with other key characters. For each one, briefly explain what the relationship shows about Romeo's character. The one for Friar Lawrence has been started for you.

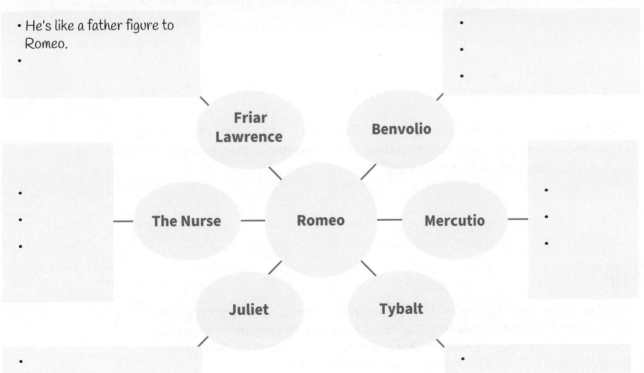

Romeo the man

Activity 5

Masculinity is a word that describes the qualities or attributes regarded as characteristic of men. When Romeo encounters Tybalt in Act 3 Scene 1, his words and actions show different ideas about what it means to be a man. In your response to an exam question on Romeo, you will need to establish an interpretation of his actions and behaviour in this **context**.

a. Look at the following interpretations of how Romeo acts in this scene and what they show about him as a man. Select examples and quotations from Act 3 Scene 1 to support each view.

   i. Romeo's impulsiveness shows his inability as a young man to control his emotions.

   ---

   ii. Romeo's obsession with love has made him soft, and he is less of a man as a result.

   ---

   iii. In contrast to the quick-tempered Mercutio, Romeo is a model of self-control.

   ---

b. Now look at Act 3 Scene 3 where Romeo discusses his banishment with Friar Lawrence. Write your own interpretation of how Romeo acts in this scene and what this shows about him as a man.

Tip

To demonstrate your wider knowledge of the play, contrast the character you are focusing on with other characters. This can allow you to explore their differences and compare how these are shown. For example, Romeo is less inclined to fight than Mercutio, but more likely to be violent than Benvolio.

The married couple in Act 3 Scene 5

Activity 6

The scene where Romeo and Juliet wake after their first night as husband and wife is a romantic scene and a direct **contrast** to Romeo's previous scenes of sword fighting in the streets of Verona and making urgent plans for escape in Friar Lawrence's cell. By switching the setting to a homely one, with Romeo and Juliet parting at dawn through her bedroom window, Shakespeare creates a dramatic contrast to heighten the intensity of the feelings he portrays.

What other linguistic, structural and dramatic methods does Shakespeare use to create a sense of Romeo's mood in this scene? The first one has been done for you.

a. a blissful, intimate mood

> The stage direction 'Enter Romeo and Juliet aloft as at the window' establishes the intimacy of the encounter as the lovers appear together. Their position above the stage reminds us of the secrecy of their love. The language they use is blissful, with natural imagery such as birds, trees, clouds and heaven, all of which have romantic connotations.

b. an ominous, threatening mood

----

c. a comic, light-hearted mood

Tip

Make references to a wide range of methods in your answers to demonstrate your understanding of Shakespeare as a dramatist. Include comments on entrances and exits, settings, sound effects, visual effects and any stage directions.

The death of Romeo in Act 5 Scene 3

Activity 7

In his last speech in Act 5 Scene 3, Romeo expresses a number of different emotions. It is the final chance for the audience to judge his character and for them to confirm how they feel about him.

a. Find quotations from this final speech where Romeo expresses the following ideas.

    i. Romeo is confused and almost regrets killing Paris, seeing him as someone else who has suffered at the hands of fate.

    ----

    ii. He wonders how it is that some men have talked of the moments before death as being cheerful.

    ----

    iii. Romeo is stunned to see how alive and beautiful Juliet looks as she lies in her tomb, as if death has no power over her.

    ----

    iv. He begs forgiveness from the corpse of Tybalt as he lies beside Juliet in the Capulet family tomb.

    ----

    v. Romeo sees his death as being a catastrophic end to an unsuccessful journey through life.

    ----

b. What impression do you get of Romeo from this final speech? Refer to examples and quotations to support your view.

Writing about Romeo – with support

Activity 8

Here is an exam-style task focusing on Romeo that provides you with an extract
from Act 3 Scene 3 to write about. Underline the key words or phrases in the task.
What precisely are you being asked to do?

> **How does the audience respond to the character of Romeo at this point in the play?**

Romeo	O thou wilt speak again of banishment.
Friar Lawrence	I'll give thee armour to keep off that word: Adversity's sweet milk, philosophy, To comfort thee though thou art banished.
Romeo	Yet 'banished'? Hang up philosophy! Unless philosophy can make a Juliet, Displant a town, reverse a prince's doom, It helps not, it prevails not; talk no more.
Friar Lawrence	O then I see that mad men have no ears.
Romeo	How should they when that wise men have no eyes?
Friar Lawrence	Let me dispute with thee of thy estate.
Romeo	Thou canst not speak of that thou dost not feel. Wert thou as young as I, Juliet thy love, An hour but married, Tybalt murdered, Doting like me, and like me banished, Then mightst thou speak, then mightst thou tear thy hair, And fall upon the ground as I do now, Taking the measure of an unmade grave.

Enter Nurse *within and knock*

Friar Lawrence	Arise, one knocks. Good Romeo, hide thyself.

Activity 9

The first stage in planning your answer is to make notes on your ideas in response
to the question. Look at the following notes that a student has made, and decide
which of these points about Romeo's character would make the best overall
argument. Highlight your choices.

Romeo's character	Audience reaction
rash	creates excitement
weak, foolish, not manly	no respect for weakness ... masculinity?
matures from boy to man by end of scene	appreciate his maturity – role of Friar
passionate about Juliet	sympathy as audience understands first love

Activity 10

When writing your answer, it's important to set out your main argument in the first paragraph. This is a one- or two-sentence summary of your response to the task.

a. Read the main argument below and underline the words and ideas that were in the student's notes in Activity 9 on page 13.

> In this scene, Shakespeare shows the maturing of Romeo from a foolish boy into a responsible man. The audience changes from having no respect for his weakness to appreciating his strength and determination.

b. Turn back to the student's notes on page 13, and in each column tick the idea the student has used as their main argument.

Activity 11

Read the opening two paragraphs of this answer to the exam-style task in Activity 8, along with the examiner's notes.

Use two different colours to underline phrases and sentences where the student supports their argument by:

a. selecting relevant references or quotations from the extract and identifying the effect of the language used

b. giving a relevant example of structure from the extract and identifying the effect of the method used.

EXCELLENT

In this scene, Shakespeare shows the maturing of Romeo from a foolish boy into a responsible man. The audience changes from having no respect for his weakness to appreciating his strength and determination. Shakespeare shows the influence of Friar Lawrence in Romeo's transformation from boy to man.

← The student has clearly set out their main argument in the introduction, indicating which big idea they are going to focus on in response to the task.

At the start of this extract, Romeo appears terrified and weak. He has just killed Tybalt and knows that he will be punished severely. Shakespeare contrasts Romeo's frantic mood: 'Yet banished?' with Friar Lawrence's calmness: 'I'll give thee armour to keep off that word'. The image of 'armour' suggests war and something hard, metal and masculine that protects you. This makes it seem like Friar Lawrence thinks Romeo needs to be manlier. Romeo continually repeats the word 'banished', as he is distressed about leaving Juliet. He repeats the word like a child would, which shows that he is immature. Shakespeare seems to show that Romeo's behaviour is unmanly and childish at the start of this scene but by the end he is more of a man.

← The student includes both structural and language points, picking up on the use of imagery and repetition. They start to make references to the big idea of masculinity.

Writing about Romeo – try it yourself

Use what you have learned to plan and write your response to this exam-style task.

> **How does the audience respond to the character of Romeo at this point in the play?**

Make a start by annotating the extract from Act 5 Scene 3 below with ideas about Romeo's character at this point in the play and the audience's reaction to him.

Romeo	Give me that mattock and the wrenching iron.
	Hold, take this letter; early in the morning
	See thou deliver it to my lord and father.
	Give me the light. Upon thy life I charge thee,
	What e'er thou hear'st or seest, stand all aloof,
	And do not interrupt me in my course.
	Why I descend into this bed of death
	Is partly to behold my lady's face,
	But chiefly to take thence from her dead finger
	A precious ring, a ring that I must use
	In dear employment; therefore hence, be gone.
	But if thou, jealous, dost return to pry
	In what I farther shall intend to do,
	By heaven, I will tear thee joint by joint,
	And strew this hungry churchyard with thy limbs.
	The time and my intents are savage-wild,
	More fierce and more inexorable far
	Than empty tigers or the roaring sea.

Activity 13

On separate paper, write your response to the exam-style task in Activity 12. You should aim to write around 500 words.

- Set out your main argument in the introductory paragraph – this should give a one- or two- sentence summary of what you are going to write in the rest of your answer.

- Stay focused on the question – make sure each paragraph is relevant and covers a key idea.

- Include references to language, structure, **stagecraft** and context by using examples, references and quotations from the extract and the rest of the play to support your points.

Juliet

Key ideas about Juliet

1. Juliet is the female **protagonist** in the play.

2. She is the daughter of Lord and Lady Capulet. Initially dutiful, Juliet later defies her parents' wishes, and her words and actions explore ideas about a daughter's role and responsibilities.

3. She is only 13 years old but shows great passion and maturity.

4. Juliet appears mostly in domestic settings and never in the street, reinforcing her lack of individual freedom.

5. Her character represents Shakespeare's views of women and womanhood, and she is seen by many as a young feminist role model.

Key quotations

'My only love sprung from my only hate!' (Juliet, Act 1 Scene 5)

'My bounty is as boundless as the sea' (Juliet, Act 2 Scene 2)

'O serpent heart, hid with a flow'ring face!' (Juliet, Act 3 Scene 2)

'O sweet my mother, cast me not away!' (Juliet, Act 3 Scene 5)

Juliet's desperation to keep her mother's love and respect falls on deaf ears as Juliet begs her not to abandon her.

'If all else fail, myself have power to die' (Juliet, Act 3 Scene 5)

Key events and structure

Act 1 Scene 3
Juliet is informed by Lady Capulet that she is to be married by arrangement to Paris.

Act 1 Scene 5
She meets Romeo at a family party, falls in love and kisses him.

Act 2 Scene 2
Juliet meets Romeo on her balcony, later the same night, and they agree to marry. The balcony **symbolises** Juliet's position on the cusp of womanhood, poised between child and adult.

Act 2 Scene 5
With the Nurse, Juliet plots her secret marriage to Romeo.

Act 3 Scene 5
Juliet bids farewell to Romeo after they spend the night together as husband and wife. Refusing her parents' demand that she marry Paris, Juliet then rejects the Nurse for advising her to abandon Romeo.

Act 4 Scene 3
Juliet takes the potion given to her by the Friar to make it seem as if she has died.

Act 5 Scene 3
Juliet wakes in her tomb to find Romeo dead beside her; she picks up a knife and kills herself.

Exploring Juliet
First impressions in Act 1

Activity 1

The audience first meets Juliet in Act 1 Scene 3 as Lady Capulet tells her daughter and the Nurse about Paris's proposal of marriage.

a. What impression do you get of Juliet in this scene? Complete the table by finding quotations from the scene to support each statement.

Statement	Quotation
Juliet is obedient and respects her mother.	
Juliet has not thought much about marriage.	
Juliet is willing to be guided by her mother's will.	

b. Why do you think it is important that Shakespeare presents Juliet in this way at the start of the play?

----

c. In Act 1 Scene 3, Juliet speaks very little, and what she says is relatively formal, reflecting her relationship with her mother, Lady Capulet. Now look at how Juliet talks to the Nurse at the ball in Act 1 Scene 5. How does this affect the audience's impression of Juliet?

Tip

Remember that characters like Juliet are not real people. Everything they say and do is deliberately created by Shakespeare for a particular effect. You should always write about characters as being presented in a specific way, not as if they are real.

Juliet and the language of love

Activity 2

Imagery is often used by writers to represent abstract ideas or emotions. As she stands on her balcony in Act 2 Scene 2, Juliet's language becomes richer and more passionate as she uses imagery to express the new emotions she is feeling.

a. Look at the quotations in the table below. For each one, explain the effect of the imagery used and what this suggests about Juliet's emotions.

Quotation	Explanation
'O swear not by the moon, th'inconstant moon, That monthly changes in her circl'd orb, Lest that thy love prove likewise variable.'	
'This bud of love, by summer's ripening breath, May prove a beauteous flower when next we meet.'	
'My bounty is as boundless as the sea, My love as deep; the more I give to thee The more I have, for both are infinite.'	

Tip

When writing about language, explore the links between the image and what it represents. For example, explain how the moon is like love. What do they have in common? What does the moon tell us about the nature of love?

b. Summarise the different ideas about love that are presented in this scene. You might want to look back at Activity 3 on page 8 to compare Juliet's views with Romeo's.

The passion of Juliet in Act 3 Scene 2

Activity 3

In Act 3 Scene 2, as Juliet waits for Romeo to come to her on their wedding night, she speaks her thoughts and desires aloud.

a. Annotate the speech below to show your understanding of Juliet's thoughts and feelings and the language she uses to express them.

Addresses the night directly, personifying it, like a fellow conspirator, reflecting the secrecy and thrill. ⟶

> Gallop apace, you fiery-footed steeds,
> Towards Phoebus' lodging; such a waggoner
> As Phaëton would whip you to the west,
> And bring in cloudy night immediately.
> Spread thy close curtain, love-performing Night,
> That runaways' eyes may wink, and Romeo
> Leap to these arms, untalk'd of and unseen:
> Lovers can see to do their amorous rites
> By their own beauties, or if love be blind,
> It best agrees with night. Come, civil Night,
> Thou sober-suited matron all in black,
> And learn me how to lose a winning match,
> Play'd for a pair of stainless maidenhoods.
> Hood my unmann'd blood, bating in my cheeks,
> With thy black mantle, till strange love grow bold,
> Think true love acted simple modesty.

b. Summarise how Juliet's emotions change after the Nurse brings news of Tybalt's death and Romeo's banishment.

----

c. Explain why you think Shakespeare has structured the scene in this way.

Juliet's relationship with her parents

Act 3 Scene 5 is a critical scene that transforms Juliet's relationship with her parents. When Lady Capulet first arrives to tell Juliet she is to be married to Paris, Juliet is weeping about losing Romeo, but her parents believe that she is tearful about Tybalt's death. This is an example of **dramatic irony**.

a. Find another example of dramatic irony in the scene.

---

b. On the chart below, map the key moments from the scene that show the rising conflict between Juliet and her parents. Think about what the characters say and do and how other characters react to this. One example has been completed for you.

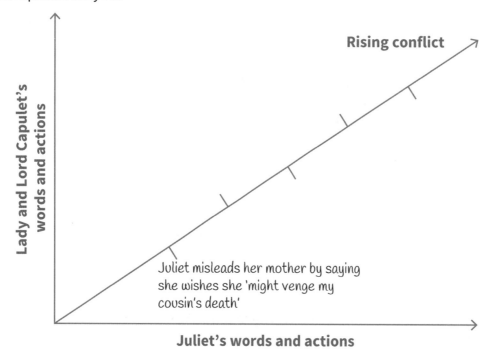

Juliet misleads her mother by saying she wishes she 'might venge my cousin's death'

Juliet's words and actions

> **Tip**
>
> Asking questions and considering the context of events can help you to explore the causes of conflict and tension. For example, why might the news of Tybalt's death have brought Juliet and her family together? How does Romeo's involvement in Tybalt's death complicate matters for Juliet?

c. Do you consider Lord and Lady Capulet's treatment of Juliet to be fair or brutal? Give reasons for your answer.

Juliet – a feminist role model?

Activity 5

Abandoned by Romeo, rejected by her parents, betrayed by the Nurse, Juliet stands alone at the end of Act 3. A weaker character might crumble, but Juliet's actions in Act 4 mean that many view her as a feminist role model, as she makes independent decisions and acts on her own judgement.

a. The following terms can help you to explain the interpretation of Juliet's character as a feminist role model. Match each term on the left with the correct definition in the column on the right. The first one has been done for you.

Term	Definition
Feminism	A social system in which men hold power
Sexism	A situation where people are dominated or overpowered
Patriarchy	The belief that men and women should be equal
Autonomy	Prejudice or discrimination based on gender
Equality	The ability to make your own choices
Oppression	Being equal, in status, rights and opportunities

b. Using at least three of the terms above, explain how Juliet takes control of her life in Act 4.

Think about:

• how she seeks advice from Friar Lawrence in Act 4 Scene 1

• how she acts when she returns home in Act 4 Scene 2

• the way she struggles with her final decision in Act 4 Scene 3.

c. Do you think Juliet is a feminist role model? Give reasons for your answer.

Final interpretations

Activity 6

As the play ends in Act 5 Scene 3 with the tragic deaths of Romeo and Juliet, the audience is left to consider their impressions of Juliet's character.

a. Consider the following different views of the character of Juliet. For each one, find quotations from the play to support this interpretation.

> Juliet is too young to know her own heart or mind. She acts impulsively, bringing about her own downfall as a result of her foolish immaturity.

> Juliet should be devoted to her family but shows them only disrespect. She fails to honour the death of her cousin or her parents' wishes in marrying Paris.

> Juliet matures rapidly through the course of the play. She demonstrates her independence and autonomy as she faces huge moral dilemmas.

----

b. Now write your own interpretation of Juliet's character and support this with examples, references or quotations from Act 5 Scene 3 and the rest of the play.

Tip

Look backwards, forwards and sideways in the play to build your interpretation. Look back to see how the character has developed; look forward to see how the play concludes for them; and look sideways to contrast the character with other characters' actions and emotions.

Writing about Juliet – with support

Activity 7

Here is an exam-style task focusing on the character of Juliet. Underline and annotate the key words in the task. What precisely are you being asked to do?

> **How does Shakespeare present Juliet's thoughts and feelings in Acts 1 and 2?**

Activity 8

Before you begin to write an answer, you need to make notes to generate and organise your ideas.

a. Think back to Acts 1 and 2. Select two or three scenes to explore this task.

Act 2 Scene 2 – balcony scene

b. Note down the different aspects of Juliet's character that are presented in your chosen scenes.

Her passion and commitment to Romeo

c. Finally, identify some structural and language features that Shakespeare uses to present her character.

Unusual setting above the stage to emphasise the exceptional/elevated nature of their love

Activity 9

Look at the following student's interpretation of how Juliet is presented in Acts 1 and 2.

Juliet is presented as a sweet-natured and compliant girl, setting up a contrast with the rebellious and independent-minded young woman she becomes later in the play, illustrating the intense drama of growing up.

Find a quotation in the play text to support this interpretation of Juliet's character at the start of the play.

Tip

To support your points, choose quotations that are also rich with language features, where possible, to provide you with opportunities to comment on the language used.

Activity 10

To answer the exam-style task in Activity 7 on page 23, it is important to find examples of a range of methods to illustrate how and why Shakespeare has presented Juliet in this way. Read the following response to the task and annotate where the student:

a. structures the response in *paragraphs* and uses quotations to reflect each point they make

b. includes the *main argument* and *big ideas*

c. uses a *wide range of vocabulary* to make points about Juliet's character

d. references *language* and *structure* as well as *staging*

EXCELLENT

In the early stages of the play, Juliet is presented as a sweet-natured and compliant girl, setting up a contrast with the rebellious and independent-minded young woman she becomes later on, and illustrating the intense drama of growing up.

In Act 1 Scene 3, our first impression of Juliet is of an innocent child happy to accept her mother's marriage plans. Her first words are 'What is your will?', the simplicity of the monosyllables in this naïve question establishing her innocence and lack of choice. This demonstrates the constraints of life as a girl at that time in a patriarchal society where young girls were married off. Shakespeare deliberately presents Juliet's character in domestic settings, reinforcing the narrowness of her life and opportunities. Juliet's dutiful and respectful attitude is essential at this point in order for Shakespeare to create a contrast.

← This paragraph focuses on how Juliet first appears in the play: sweet-natured and compliant. The student selects just one quotation but uses it effectively to comment on the use of language.

By Act 1 Scene 5, Juliet begins to spread her wings a little. The play is structured so that she emerges from her private room into a more public world with a mix of people. Juliet is presented as exhilarated, shown in her informal dialogue with the Nurse, 'What's he that follows here ...?' She shows through her language that she is developing her own mind when she realises who Romeo is, saying 'My only love sprung from my only hate!' This exclamation shows the beginning of her passionate nature, the opposite abstract nouns 'love' and 'hate' showing the powerful extreme emotions of young people, and symbolising the main themes of the play.

By the start of Act 2 Scene 2, Juliet is trying to escape the restrictions of her life. She is moving from being a child to a woman very quickly. The scene is set on the balcony, above the normal stage, which highlights visually the possibility of freedom. Juliet is presented as having passionate feelings: 'My bounty is as boundless as the sea'. Shakespeare uses this simile to show how deep and limitless her love for Romeo is. The alliteration reinforces the enthusiasm and forcefulness of her words.

However, Juliet stays inside, symbolising that at this stage she is not fully mature. She is very modest and strong-minded when she tells Romeo 'What satisfaction canst thou have tonight?', suggesting that she is not willing to give herself to him yet. Shakespeare continues to display the maturing process as the play progresses. It is only because the audience has seen Juliet as sweet, dutiful and compliant in the early stages that they can appreciate Juliet as a mature, passionate and independent woman in the final stages of the play.

Writing about Juliet – try it yourself

Activity 11

Use what you have learned to practise writing about Juliet. Underline and annotate the key words in the exam question below. What precisely are you being asked to do?

> **How does Shakespeare present the changes in Juliet's character in Acts 3, 4 and 5?**

Activity 12

Now write a plan for the task. Follow the three stages below to plan your answer.

Stage 1 – Make notes and organise your ideas.

Stage 2 – Decide on your main argument for the introduction.

Stage 3 – Identify how to include language, structure, **stagecraft** and context.

Activity 13

On separate paper, write your response to the task in Activity 11. You should aim to write around 500 words.

- Start your essay with a clear introduction that signposts your argument.

- Stay focused on the question – make sure every paragraph is relevant.

- Use examples, references and quotations from the play to support your points.

- Refer to the choices of language and structure made by Shakespeare.

Friar Lawrence and the Nurse

Key ideas about Friar Lawrence and the Nurse

1. Friar Lawrence is a neutral character, not linked to either of the feuding families, and **symbolises** a religious perspective in the play.

2. Friar Lawrence gives advice to both Romeo and Juliet at critical points in the story.

3. The Nurse has been like a mother to Juliet for nearly 14 years but ultimately betrays Juliet and loses her trust.

4. The Nurse is involved in the play's lighter comic moments, but her role also explores ideas about the wisdom and foolishness of age, and the greater good.

5. Both the Friar and the Nurse play a significant role in the final tragedy.

Key quotations

'Wisely and slow, they stumble that run fast'
(Friar Lawrence, Act 2 Scene 3)

'These violent delights have violent ends' (Friar Lawrence, Act 2 Scene 6)

The **repetition** in the Friar's words reinforces his fear of the consequences of such a hasty and passionate love affair, and links to the theme of violence in the play.

'Will you speak well of him that kill'd your cousin?' (The Nurse, Act 3 Scene 2)

'Go, girl, seek happy nights to happy days' (The Nurse, Act 1 Scene 3)

'I think it best you married with the County' (The Nurse, Act 3 Scene 5)

Key events and structure

Act 1 Scene 3
The Nurse joins in as Juliet and Lady Capulet discuss Juliet's impending marriage.

Act 2 Scene 3
Friar Lawrence agrees to Romeo's request to secretly marry Romeo and Juliet.

Act 3 Scene 3
After Romeo kills Tybalt, Friar Lawrence plans for Romeo to flee but later reunite with Juliet.

Act 3 Scene 5
The Nurse attends Juliet as her parents try to force her marriage to Paris and advises Juliet to abandon Romeo.

Act 4 Scene 1
Friar Lawrence advises Juliet to take a sleeping potion to appear dead and avoid marrying Paris.

Act 4 Scenes 4 and 5
The Nurse tries to wake Juliet on her wedding day and is horrified to find her 'dead'.

Act 5 Scene 2
Friar Lawrence realises that Romeo has not received news of the plan for Juliet and hurries to the tomb.

Act 5 Scene 3
Friar Lawrence fails to stop Juliet's death and confesses to the gathered families his role in the tragedy.

Exploring Friar Lawrence and the Nurse
Similarities and differences

Activity 1

Despite being very different characters, the Nurse and Friar Lawrence have several features in common. Complete the table below, identifying the features the two characters share and the features that are specific to each character. Some examples have been added to get you started.

The Nurse	Friar Lawrence	Both characters
comic character	advisor to Romeo	older character, advisor to Juliet, trusted, respected

Activity 2

There are differences between the setting of the scenes where Friar Lawrence and the Nurse appear that have an impact on the **mood** and the audience's response. Complete the chart below to show these differences.

Scene	Nurse/Friar	Setting	Mood	Impact
Act 1 Scene 3	Nurse	Juliet's room	Funny, excited, intimate	Tense anticipation but comic
Act 2 Scene 3				
Act 2 Scene 4				
Act 3 Scene 5				
Act 4 Scene 1				
Act 5 Scene 3				

The role of Friar Lawrence

Friar Lawrence is an older man who works for the Church and has no allegiance to either of the feuding families. His intentions are peaceful, in line with his religious beliefs, but his words and actions influence the play's tragic outcome. In Act 2 Scene 3, Friar Lawrence is visited in his cell by Romeo.

a. What advice does Friar Lawrence give Romeo about Rosaline?

---

b. How would you describe his attitude to Romeo's news?

---

c. What is Friar Lawrence's motivation for helping Romeo to marry Juliet?

---

d. Write down three quotations where Friar Lawrence uses **imagery** related to the natural world, and explain what these suggest about his character.

---

e. How does Shakespeare create the calmer mood and slower pace of this scene? Think about the number of characters on stage; the setting of the scene; the dialogue between the characters, and how the characters leave the stage.

Tip

When exploring the role of Friar Lawrence in the play, you will need to decide if his good intentions are sufficient reason to absolve him of responsibility for the tragic events that take place.

Friar Lawrence's plan in Act 3 Scene 3

Activity 4

After the death of Tybalt, Friar Lawrence again offers Romeo advice, this time to stop him from suicidal despair at the prospect of exile from Verona. He proposes a plan to help resolve the complicated events that have taken place so suddenly since the hasty marriage between Romeo and Juliet, which he is responsible for secretly arranging.

a. Read the following speech from Act 3 Scene 3 and annotate to show where Friar Lawrence:

- encourages Romeo to see his good fortune

- rebukes Romeo for feeling such despair

- compares Romeo to a sulky woman

- instructs Romeo to spend his wedding night with Juliet

- warns Romeo not to stay too long

- is optimistic about the outcome of his plan.

b. Using different colours, highlight any examples of repetition, **personification**, **hyperbole**, **imperatives** and **similes** in the speech.

What, rouse thee, man! thy Juliet is alive,

For whose dear sake thou wast but lately dead:

There art thou happy. Tybalt would kill thee,

But thou slewest Tybalt: there art thou happy.

The law that threaten'd death becomes thy friend, ← Friar Lawrence encourages Romeo to see his good fortune.

And turns it to exile: there art thou happy.

A pack of blessings light upon thy back,

Happiness courts thee in her best array,

But like a mishaved and sullen wench,

Thou pouts upon thy fortune and thy love:

Take heed, take heed, for such die miserable.

Go get thee to thy love as was decreed,

Ascend her chamber, hence and comfort her;

But look thou stay not till the Watch be set,

For then thou canst not pass to Mantua,

Where thou shalt live till we can find a time

To blaze your marriage, reconcile your friends,

Beg pardon of the prince, and call thee back

With twenty hundred thousand times more joy

Than thou went'st forth in lamentation.

First impressions of the Nurse

The Nurse is a memorable and popular character in the play, much loved by Juliet and audiences alike. However, she is not perhaps all that she seems at first, and the development of her character is significant. We first meet the Nurse in conversation with Lady Capulet and Juliet in Act 1 Scene 3.

a. Explain what each of the following quotations from this scene tells us about the character of the Nurse. Comment on the language she uses, where appropriate.

Quotation	What this tells us about the Nurse
'What, lamb! What, ladybird!'	
'Faith, I can tell her age unto an hour.'	
'Yes, madam, yet I cannot choose but laugh, To think it should leave crying, and say "Ay"'	
'Thou wast the prettiest babe that e'er I nurs'd.'	
'Go, girl, seek happy nights to happy days.'	

b. What impression does Act 1 Scene 5 (the masked ball scene) give you of the Nurse's relationship with Juliet? How does this compare with Juliet's relationship with her own mother, Lady Capulet?

The Nurse's actions and attitudes

Activity 6

As the play progresses, the Nurse encourages Juliet's relationship with Romeo. However, when Romeo kills Tybalt and is banished, she changes her attitude completely and advises Juliet to marry Paris.

a. Complete the table below, finding evidence that shows how the Nurse's actions and attitude change during the play.

At first, the Nurse …	Evidence	By the end, the Nurse …	Evidence
is loyal to Juliet		is loyal to Juliet's parents	
is trustworthy		is traitorous	
is comical		is grief-stricken	
is keen to help Juliet		refuses to help Juliet	
supports Juliet's independence		supports Juliet's compliance	

b. Explain how the Nurse's attitude towards Juliet changes throughout the play. You should refer to examples from the play to support your explanation.

Who is responsible?

Both Friar Lawrence and the Nurse must bear some responsibility for the tragedy of Romeo and Juliet's deaths. You need to interpret their characters in this **context**, and decide how you think Shakespeare wanted audiences to respond.

a. Read the following interpretations, and circle which you feel is best supported by the text.

The Friar	The Nurse
Very good intentions, but events unfortunately got in the way – not responsible	Kind, caring, committed and pragmatic – not responsible
Meddling, foolish, idealistic and not realistic – partially responsible	Unable to empathise with Juliet due to age/class – partially responsible
Self-centred, arrogant, secretive and should have known better – entirely responsible	Selfish, concerned with own position, betrays Juliet – entirely responsible

b. Select evidence to support your chosen interpretation of one of these characters. See how this has been done for the first interpretation of Friar Lawrence.

> Friar Lawrence is not responsible for the tragic deaths of the lovers, because he did everything he could to save them. He supported their marriage in the hopes of bringing peace to Verona, and advised Romeo when he was banished. It was not his fault that Juliet's marriage with Paris was arranged or that the letter informing Romeo about the plan for Juliet's 'death' did not arrive in time.

Tip

The word 'responsible' can have different meanings. To be *responsible* is to act sensibly and with consideration; to be *responsible for* something is to be held to account for your actions. This question is asking you to think about both meanings.

Writing about Friar Lawrence – with support

Activity 8

Here is an exam-style task focusing on the character of Friar Lawrence. Underline and annotate the key words in the task. What precisely are you being asked to do?

> **How far do the words and actions of Friar Lawrence make him responsible for the tragic outcome of the play?**

Activity 9

Here is a student's plan for the task in Activity 8. They have taken three of Friar Lawrence's actions and noted what type of responsibility this shows.

Partly responsible

- Advising R & J and marrying them – socially irresponsible

- Juliet's 'death' causes grief to Capulets – morally irresponsible

- Thinks he can bring peace – religiously irresponsible

Look back at Activity 7 on page 32, and choose one of the other interpretations of the Friar's character as the starting point for an essay. Make notes on Friar Lawrence's words and actions, and identify whether they make him responsible or irresponsible.

Activity 10

When writing an essay, make sure that each quotation or example you use offers the opportunity to comment on language, structure or **stagecraft**. Annotate each of the quotations or examples below to identify what it tells us about Friar Lawrence, the methods used and their effects.

Setting many of Friar Lawrence's scene in his cell

'Wisely and slow, they stumble that run fast.' (Friar Lawrence, Act 2 Scene 3)

'With twenty hundred thousand times more joy' (Friar Lawrence, Act 3 Scene 3)

'let my old life be sacrific'd' (Friar Lawrence, Act 5 Scene 3)

Activity 11

Read the following good response to the task in Activity 8, along with the examiner's notes.

Use four different colours to underline phrases and sentences where the student has:

a. made three clear points

b. referred to the task

c. commented on the language and structure

d. referred to the big ideas.

GOOD

Friar Lawrence is partly to blame for the outcome of the play. His actions demonstrate irresponsible behaviour that has unintended consequences. He is morally, socially and religiously irresponsible, and this leads directly or indirectly to the deaths of the two people he tries so hard to help.

Friar Lawrence is religiously irresponsible as he agrees to marry two people who have only just met. Shakespeare sets most of the Friar's scenes in his cell, which has a calmer mood and slower pace than the party and street scenes. It is a visual and structural reminder that Friar Lawrence's character is also set apart from the world. He is idealistic, believing that he can create peace in the outside world from the safety of his cell. This is not realistic, and may represent Shakespeare's view that the Church is too focused on ideals and good intentions and doesn't understand real life.

← The student clearly refers to the Friar's perceived responsibilities as a member of the Church and therefore perceived irresponsibility in marrying the lovers so quickly. Big ideas of idealism and religion are included accurately.

Friar Lawrence is socially irresponsible to use people's lives to try to create a peaceful and harmonious society. This possibility of peace occurs to him immediately when Romeo tells him that he has fallen in love with a Capulet, but he doesn't consider the consequences. He warns Romeo not to be hasty: 'Wisely and slow, they stumble that run fast.' The Friar's language sounds like a proverb from the Bible, reinforcing his Christian perspective and suggesting the idea of the play as a parable. It also emphasises his age and supposed wisdom.

He is also morally irresponsible to abuse people's trust, when both young protagonists have faith in him, and forfeit their lives as a result. Equally, to allow Juliet's family to believe she is dead and bury her is unforgivably cruel. He is short-sighted and blinded by one purpose. The play is a moral lesson about our responsibility to family, friends and society as a whole. He persuades Romeo to go into exile with the promise that he will return 'With twenty hundred thousand times more joy' – the hyperbole emphasises his idealistic optimism that all will be forgiven.

Friar Lawrence realises his fatal errors too late. He recognises that he is very much to blame, but he is pardoned by the Prince, who is the voice of moral authority. Friar Lawrence ends the play humbled by the Prince, having attempted to play God himself by trying to bring peace, at which he succeeds to some extent, but at a terrible cost.

Writing about the Nurse – try it yourself

Use what you have learned to plan and write your response to the exam question below.

> **How far is the Nurse responsible for the tragic outcome of the play?**

a. Start planning your response by writing a chronological list of the Nurse's actions and their consequences.

---

b. Decide on your main argument for the introduction. You could look back at Activity 7 on page 32, but try to develop your own interpretation.

---

c. Consider how to include language, structure, stagecraft and **context**. Choose quotations or examples from relevant scenes in the play and make notes on the methods used and their effects.

On separate paper, write your response to the task in Activity 12. You should aim to write around 500 words.

- Start your essay with a clear introduction that signposts your argument.

- Stay focused on the question – make sure every paragraph is relevant.

- Use examples, references and quotations from the play to support your points.

- Refer to the choices of language and structure made by Shakespeare.

Lord and Lady Capulet

Key ideas about Lord and Lady Capulet

1. Lord Capulet is the head of the Capulet family and a figure of authority.

2. He appears fond of his daughter, Juliet, but arranges her marriage to Paris and threatens to disown her when she defies him.

3. Lady Capulet's relationship with her daughter is cool and distant, and she relies on the Nurse in her conversations with Juliet.

4. Lady Capulet was married young herself and as a woman in the play appears to have little freedom or independence, despite her status.

5. Lord and Lady Capulet represent the older generation and embody ideas about parental love and responsibility, loyalty, honour and power.

Key quotations

'Am I the master here, or you?' (Lord Capulet, Act 1 Scene 5)

'How, will she none? doth she not give us thanks?' (Lord Capulet, Act 3 Scene 5)

'Speak briefly, can you like of Paris' love?' (Lady Capulet, Act 1 Scene 3)

'I would the fool were married to her grave.' (Lady Capulet, Act 3 Scene 5)

'O brother Montague, give me thy hand.' (Lord Capulet, Act 5 Scene 3)

Lady Capulet rejects her daughter entirely, cursing her to death, demonstrating her cold-hearted attitude.

Key events and structure

Act 1 Scene 1
Lord and Lady Capulet appear at the scene of the fight, with Lord Capulet calling for his sword, but Lady Capulet reminds him of his age.

Act 1 Scene 2
Paris asks Lord Capulet's permission to marry Juliet, but he refuses, saying that his daughter is too young.

Act 1 Scene 3
Lady Capulet asks Juliet if she is willing to marry Paris.

Act 1 Scene 5
Lord Capulet welcomes guests to his ball and insists that Tybalt allow Romeo to stay.

Act 3 Scene 5
Lord and Lady Capulet confront Juliet about her refusal to marry Paris. In this scene, there is a clear **contrast** between Lord Capulet's good temper and his anger.

Act 4 Scene 5
Lord and Lady Capulet, among others, find Juliet 'dead' on the morning of her wedding to Paris.

Act 5 Scene 3
Lord and Lady Capulet arrive at the tomb to hear, too late, the story of Romeo and Juliet. Their presence in the first and last scenes shows a circular structure and **symbolises** the structural shift from violence to truce.

Exploring Lord and Lady Capulet
The many faces of Lord Capulet

Lord Capulet is introduced in Act 1 Scene 1 as a faintly ridiculous character, wearing a nightgown and calling for a sword to join the fighting in the streets. The stage direction refers to him as 'old Capulet' which, alongside his appearance in this scene, suggests the audience might respond with laughter at his foolish aggression rather than with respect for his age and wisdom.

a. Now look at Lord Capulet's meeting with Paris in Act 1 Scene 2, when Paris asks his permission to marry Juliet. Explain what Lord Capulet's response suggests about him as a father.

----

b. Read the following extract from Act 1 Scene 5, where Lord Capulet asserts his authority when Tybalt threatens to disturb the lively, but peaceful **mood** of the party. Annotate the extract to show the different emotions shown by Lord Capulet.

Tybalt	Uncle, this is a Montague, our foe: A villain that is hither come in spite, To scorn at our solemnity this night.
Lord Capulet	Young Romeo is it?
Tybalt	'Tis he, that villain Romeo.
Lord Capulet	Content thee, gentle coz, let him alone, 'A bears him like a portly gentleman; And to say truth, Verona brags of him To be a virtuous and well-govern'd youth. I would not for the wealth of all this town Here in my house do him disparagement; Therefore be patient, take no note of him; It is my will, the which if thou respect, Show a fair presence, and put off these frowns, An ill-beseeming semblance for a feast.
Tybalt	It fits when such a villain is a guest: I'll not endure him.
Lord Capulet	He shall be endur'd. What, goodman boy, I say he shall, go to! Am I the master here, or you? go to! You'll not endure him? God shall mend my soul, You'll make a mutiny among my guests! You will set cock-a-hoop! you'll be the man!
Tybalt	Why, uncle, 'tis a shame.

Lord Capulet recognises Romeo calmly, as if he is the boy next door, not a hated enemy.

c. What does this dialogue between Tybalt and Lord Capulet tell us about the older man's character? Think about why he responds so calmly to start with, and how his emotions change as the conversation progresses.

A changeable man

Nowhere is Lord Capulet's volatile character shown better than in his changing relationship with his daughter Juliet.

a. Look back at the scenes these characters share and find quotations to support the following descriptions of Lord Capulet's feelings about Juliet.

Lord Capulet's feelings	Quotation
his concern for Juliet's wellbeing as he arranges her marriage	
his dismissal of her feelings as she mourns her cousin's death	
his fury with her for refusing to cooperate	
his delight when Juliet appears to change her mind	
his despair when he believes she has died	

b. Summarise your overall impression of Lord Capulet's relationship with Juliet.

Lady Capulet revealed

Activity 3

Like her husband, Lady Capulet is also passionate and demonstrates a wide range of emotions throughout the play. However, there are also times when she struggles to show her feelings.

a. Read the quotations below and identify which show Lady Capulet's strong feelings and which show her being more restrained. Write either 'strong feelings' or 'restrained' next to each quotation to describe Lady Capulet's emotions.

'A crutch, a crutch! why call you for a sword?' (Act 1 Scene 1)

'Speak briefly, can you like of Paris' love?' (Act 1 Scene 3)

'Some grief shows much of love,
But much of grief shows still some want of wit.' (Act 3 Scene 5)

'We will have vengeance for it, fear thou not' (Act 3 Scene 5)

'Talk not to me, for I'll not speak a word.' (Act 3 Scene 5)

'Accurs'd, unhappy, wretched, hateful day!' (Act 4 Scene 5)

b. Write a summary of what this contrast tells us about Lady Capulet's emotions. Consider her position as the wife of a powerful man. Does Lady Capulet appear to have similar power and influence? If not, why not?

Tip

It is not always clear how Shakespeare intended dialogue to be spoken. For example, Lady Capulet's promise to revenge Tybalt's death could be a cold, hard, quiet determination, or a wild, passionate scream of agony. It is up to you to interpret the text and consider alternative ways of performing the character's words.

Lady Capulet: a good parent?

Lady Capulet is commonly thought to be considerably younger than her husband, and declares that she herself was married at a similar age to Juliet. As a mother, Lady Capulet seems intent on her daughter following the same traditional path of arranged marriage rather than supporting her to make different choices.

a. Complete the table below with the words and actions that relate to Lady Capulet's role as a parent. Add comments to summarise what this tells us about her character. One example has been done for you.

Lady Capulet's words or actions	What this tells us
Discusses marriage with Juliet	Lady Capulet is keen to create a closer bond with Juliet by talking to her about Paris.

b. Summarise how far you think Lady Capulet is presented as a good parent.

Lord and Lady Capulet versus Juliet

Activity 5

There are several scenes featuring Lord and Lady Capulet and their daughter during the play that allow the audience to judge their family relationship. The most important of these is Act 3 Scene 5, where both parents confront Juliet about her refusal to marry Paris. In this dramatic scene, Shakespeare provides several indications in the dialogue to suggest how he intended the characters to act.

a. What clues are there in the following quotations about how the characters might act, move about or interact in this scene?

   i. **'What are they, beseech your ladyship?'** (Juliet)

   ii. **'Here comes your father, tell him so yourself'** (Lady Capulet)

   iii. **'Soft, take me with you, take me with you, wife.'** (Lord Capulet)

   iv. **'Or I will drag thee on a hurdle thither.'** (Lord Capulet)

   v. **'Fie, fie, what, are you mad?'** (Lady Capulet)

   vi. **'Good father, I beseech you on my knees'** (Juliet)

   vii. **'Do as thou wilt, for I have done with thee'** (Lady Capulet)

b. What do you notice about the language in these quotations? Why do you think Shakespeare used such simple language at these points?

Judging Lord and Lady Capulet

Activity 6

Lord and Lady Capulet's words and actions as people and parents are painfully exposed by the play's tragic outcome, and the audience is invited by Shakespeare to judge their successes and their failures.

a. Which of the following statements best summarises your view of Lord Capulet? Circle your choice.

- Lord Capulet is a dangerous man; he is emotionally volatile, verbally vicious and potentially violent.

- As a loving and considerate father, Lord Capulet goes to extraordinary lengths to find his daughter a suitable husband.

- Lord Capulet can be forgiven for his more extreme actions as he is motivated purely to protect his family honour.

b. Explain your choice of statement. Support your explanation with examples, references or quotations from the rest of the play.

----

c. Which of the following statements best summarises your view of Lady Capulet? Circle your choice.

- Lady Capulet is aware of the distance between her and her daughter, and she does all she can to create a closer bond by arranging Juliet's marriage.

- Lady Capulet is so blinded by the limitations of her own life that she totally fails to support her daughter's desire for independence.

- Her reaction to the death of Juliet shows just how dearly Lady Capulet loved her daughter but was unable to express her emotions while Juliet was alive.

d. Explain your choice of statement. Support your explanation with examples, references or quotations from the rest of the play.

Writing about Lady Capulet – with support

Activity 7

Here is an exam-style task focusing on Lady Capulet that provides you with an extract from the play to write about. Underline and annotate the key words or phrases in the task. What precisely are you being asked to do?

> **Consider how Shakespeare presents Lady Capulet's relationship with Juliet in this extract from Act 3 Scene 5.**

Activity 8

Look at the annotations the following student has made on the extract from Act 3 Scene 5 to help them answer the task. Add your own notes to identify:

- the **characteristics** of Lady Capulet

- the characteristics of Juliet's response

- how big ideas or themes are explored in the presentation of their relationship.

Lady Capulet	Marry, my child, early next Thursday morn, The gallant, young, and noble gentleman, The County Paris, at Saint Peter's Church, Shall happily make thee there a joyful bride.	
Juliet	Now by Saint Peter's Church and Peter too, He shall not make me there a joyful bride. I wonder at this haste, that I must wed Ere he that should be husband comes to woo. I pray you tell my lord and father, madam, I will not marry yet, and when I do, I swear It shall be Romeo, whom you know I hate, Rather than Paris. These are news indeed!	← Juliet is determined not to marry Paris. ← A challenge to male authority
Lady Capulet	Here comes your father, tell him so yourself; And see how he will take it at your hands.	← Shows Lady Capulet's frustration with Juliet

Enter Lord Capulet *and* Nurse

Activity 9

Read this good response to the exam-style task in Activity 7 on page 43.

Use four different colours to underline phrases and sentences where the student has commented on:

a. Lady Capulet's character in relation to Juliet

b. big ideas such as feminism, parenting, control, etc.

c. Shakespeare's language

d. use of structural and other dramatic devices.

Lady Capulet is so blinded by the limitations of her own life that she totally fails to support her daughter's desire for independence. In this scene, Lady Capulet tries to persuade her daughter to marry Paris, even though she has suffered the same fate of being married off as a teenager. She cannot see that Juliet could make different choices and be happier.

Lady Capulet persuades Juliet using hyperbole, to exaggerate the benefits of being 'a joyful bride'. She describes Paris using a triplet, 'The gallant, young, and noble gentleman', which builds up an image of a desirable and attractive proposition for Juliet. The optimistic language is a contrast with the mood in this scene to this point, which began with the passionate love between Romeo and Juliet, and grief for the death of Tybalt. Shakespeare creates these contrasts to highlight the link between death and love.

Lady Capulet doesn't try very hard to persuade Juliet or to understand her feelings. She quickly gives up and passes responsibility to her husband. She says, 'Here comes your father, tell him so yourself.' The sudden entrance of Lord Capulet at this point reinforces the dominance of her husband and Lady Capulet's subservient position (she calls him 'Sir'). It is likely that she knows exactly how Lord Capulet will react and she does nothing to protect or side with her daughter. There is no empathy in Lady Capulet's language, which is simple, cold and hard. Lord Capulet takes centre stage to berate his daughter, and Lady Capulet willingly steps back, metaphorically and possibly also visually, on stage.

The relationship between Lady Capulet and her daughter has been distant and formal ← since their opening scene, where Lady Capulet struggled to engage with Juliet. Later, when Juliet appears dead, Lady Capulet is terribly upset, suggesting that she does care for her, but in this pivotal scene in Act 3, Lady Capulet fails the parenting test: she betrays her daughter by leaving her at the mercy of her potentially violent husband. She rejects her, saying 'I would the fool were married to her grave.' The metaphor extends the motifs of death and love that are woven throughout the play, and it foreshadows the final scene, where Romeo and Juliet lie together in death as if on their marriage bed. It is almost a curse on Juliet.

If Juliet is seen by some audiences as Shakespeare's feminist role model, because of her confidence, independence and determination, Lady Capulet represents the opposite, as she betrays her daughter's trust, bowing to the authority of her husband and failing to support Juliet's attempt to assert her own independence in life.

In this paragraph, the student develops their response beyond the extract, looking back to compare Lady Capulet's early relationship with Juliet and forward to how she reacts to her death, demonstrating a broader knowledge of the play. The student also draws on the big ideas of parental love and the absence of it here, and successfully links this with a comment on language in the analysis of the 'marriage/grave' image.

Writing about Lord Capulet – try it yourself

Activity 10

Use what you have learned to plan and write your response to this exam-style task.

> **Consider how Shakespeare presents Lord Capulet's relationship with Juliet in this extract from Act 3 Scene 5.**

Lord Capulet	[...] How now, wife,
	Have you deliver'd to her our decree?
Lady Capulet	Ay, sir, but she will none, she gives you thanks.
	I would the fool were married to her grave.
Lord Capulet	Soft, take me with you, take me with you, wife.
	How, will she none? doth she not give us thanks?
	Is she not proud? doth she not count her blest,
	Unworthy as she is, that we have wrought
	So worthy a gentleman to be her bride?
Juliet	Not proud you have, but thankful that you have:
	Proud can I never be of what I hate,
	But thankful even for hate that is meant love.
Lord Capulet	How how, how how, chopt-logic? What is this?
	'Proud', and 'I thank you', and 'I thank you not',
	And yet 'not proud', mistress minion you?
	Thank me no thankings, nor proud me no prouds,
	But fettle your fine joints 'gainst Thursday next,
	To go with Paris to Saint Peter's Church,
	Or I will drag thee on a hurdle thither.
	Out, you green-sickness carrion! out, you baggage!
	You tallow-face!

a. Annotate the extract to identify the characteristics of Lord Capulet and Juliet, and the big ideas or themes that are explored in their relationship.

b. Then highlight examples of language, structure, **stagecraft** and **context** you could refer to in your answer.

Activity 11

On separate paper, write your response to the task in Activity 10. You should aim to write around 500 words.

- Start your essay with a clear introduction that signposts your argument.

- Stay focused on the question – make sure every paragraph is relevant.

- Use examples, references and quotations from the extract and the rest of the play to support your points.

- Refer to the choices of language and structure made by Shakespeare.

Tybalt and Mercutio

Key ideas about Tybalt and Mercutio

1. Tybalt is a Capulet and Juliet's cousin.

2. Tybalt's loyalty to his family leads to violence and conflict.

3. Mercutio is one of Romeo's closest friends. However, as a relation of the Prince, he is not directly involved in the family feud.

4. Mercutio can be comic, poetic, lewd or deadly serious and has long been a favourite with audiences.

5. As young men full of energy and passion, Tybalt and Mercutio embody different aspects of masculinity. Their words and actions explore ideas of honour and dishonour.

Key quotations

'What, drawn and talk of peace?' (Tybalt, Act 1 Scene 1)

'Now by the stock and honour of my kin,
To strike him dead I hold it not a sin.' (Tybalt, Act 1 Scene 5)

'O calm, dishonourable, vile submission!'
(Mercutio, Act 3 Scene 1)

These words highlight Mercutio's fury at Romeo's cowardice in refusing to fight Tybalt, provoking a deadly battle on the streets.

'If love be rough with you, be rough with love' (Mercutio, Act 1 Scene 4)

'A plague a'both houses!' (Mercutio, Act 3 Scene 1)

Key events and structure

Act 1 Scene 1
Tybalt and other Capulets fight members of the Montague family in the street. Tybalt is key to the early scenes of violence and conflict between the two families.

Act 1 Scene 4
Mercutio and Benvolio persuade Romeo to attend the Capulet party.

Act 1 Scene 5
Tybalt recognises Romeo at the masked ball and seeks to attack him, but is stopped by Lord Capulet. Tybalt's appearance on stage is always accompanied by violence or the threat of it.

Act 2 Scene 4
Mercutio teases the Nurse in the streets in a comic scene. Mercutio's exits and entrances reinforce his unpredictable, volatile character.

Act 3 Scene 1
Tybalt and Mercutio die within minutes of each other, in the same central scene of vengeance and violence. Mercutio, outraged by Romeo's refusal to meet Tybalt's challenge, fights and is killed by Tybalt, as Romeo and Benvolio try to stop them. Romeo blames himself for Mercutio's death and seeks revenge by killing Tybalt.

Exploring Tybalt and Mercutio
Tybalt, king of cats

Tybalt's aggression and attitude towards violence are established from the very first scene. Look at his words as he joins the fighting in Act 1 Scene 1.

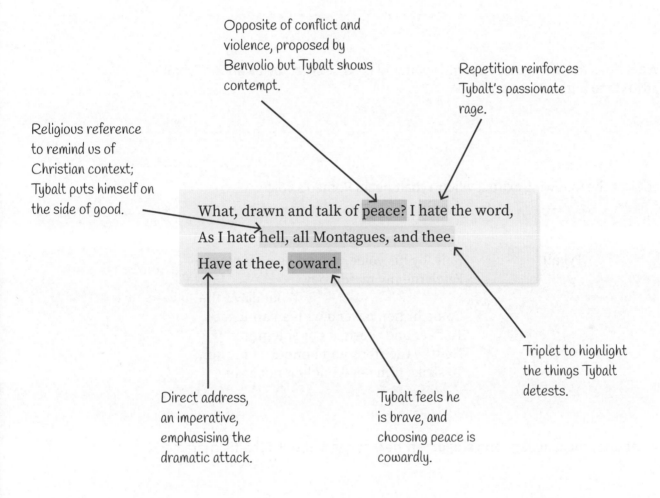

Opposite of conflict and violence, proposed by Benvolio but Tybalt shows contempt.

Repetition reinforces Tybalt's passionate rage.

Religious reference to remind us of Christian context; Tybalt puts himself on the side of good.

What, drawn and talk of peace? I hate the word,

As I hate hell, all Montagues, and thee.

Have at thee, coward.

Triplet to highlight the things Tybalt detests.

Direct address, an imperative, emphasising the dramatic attack.

Tybalt feels he is brave, and choosing peace is cowardly.

Explain how Shakespeare's use of language portrays Tybalt's attitude to violence.

Antagonism in Act 1 Scene 5

Activity 2

Tybalt is Romeo's **antagonist** in the play. In Act 1 Scene 5, as the masked ball is in full swing, Tybalt recognises Romeo's voice as being that of a Montague.

a. How does Shakespeare use Tybalt's response to seeing Romeo to create a contrast in mood in this scene?

----

b. What does the dialogue between Tybalt and Lord Capulet tell us about Tybalt's attitude to authority?

----

c. Look at the following extract when Tybalt hears Romeo's voice.

> Tybalt
>
> This, by his voice, should be a Montague.
> Fetch me my rapier, boy.   [Exit Page
>   What dares the slave
> Come hither, cover'd with an antic face,
> To fleer and scorn at our solemnity?
> Now by the stock and honour of my kin,
> To strike him dead I hold it not a sin.

What does the language and **stagecraft** here suggest about Tybalt's character?

----

d. How does this minor event involving Tybalt at the party **foreshadow** the final tragedy of the play?

----

e. Tybalt is linked to the idea of death in this extract. How does Tybalt justify his threat to kill Romeo?

Mercutio – a complex character

Mercutio first appears with his friends, as he does in every scene, firmly establishing that his loyalty is to friends rather than family. He is often portrayed as wild and excitable or rude and comedic, but there is a sensitive, poetic side to Mercutio too.

a. Complete the table below to show where Mercutio demonstrates these different **characteristics**. The first row has been completed for you.

Characteristic	Example	Act/Scene
obscene	Teases the Nurse with mocking sexual references	Act 2 Scene 4
stubborn		
principled		
loyal		
witty		
volatile		
brave		
poetic		

b. Summarise your impression of the contrasts in Mercutio's character.

Mercutio – love and friendship

Activity 4

a. What does each of the following quotations tell us about Mercutio's views on love? The first one has been done for you.

   i. 'I conjure thee by Rosaline's bright eyes,
      By her high forehead and her scarlet lip' (Act 2 Scene 1)

   > He mocks Romeo's devotion to Rosaline and tries to persuade him away from her.

   ii. 'If love be rough with you, be rough with love:
       Prick love for pricking, and you beat love down.' (Act 1 Scene 4)

   ----

   iii. 'If love be blind, love cannot hit the mark.' (Act 2 Scene 1)

   ----

   iv. 'Alas, poor Romeo, he is already dead, stabbed with a white wench's
       black eye, run through the ear with a love-song, the very pin of his heart
       cleft with the blind bow-boy's butt-shaft' (Act 2 Scene 4)

   ----

b. Write a sentence summarising Mercutio's views on love.

   ----

c. Explain how Shakespeare uses Mercutio's attitude to love as a contrast with Romeo's. You should comment on:

   - how serious or humorous they are about love
   - how frequently we see them with women
   - how sensitive they seem
   - what aspects of love they talk about most.

Tybalt versus Mercutio

Activity 5

In Act 3 Scene 1, the violence of the play is heightened with the fights between Tybalt and Mercutio, and then Romeo and Tybalt. The feud between the families that has simmered below the surface and threatened to break out finally explodes in a fatal confrontation between three of the main characters, two of whom end up dead.

a. Number these statements 1 to 10 to show the chronology of events in this scene, from first to last. Find a quotation to support each statement.

Number	Statement	Quotation
	Mercutio curses the two families.	
	Mercutio wants to provoke a fight with Tybalt.	
	Romeo is keen to avoid a fight with Tybalt.	
	Tybalt has no intention of fighting Mercutio.	
	Benvolio is concerned that a fight might start.	
	Mercutio is frustrated by Romeo's refusal to fight.	
	Romeo is distressed to see Mercutio fight Tybalt.	
	Tybalt wants revenge on Romeo.	
	Romeo seeks revenge on Tybalt for Mercutio's death.	
	Romeo tries to stop the fight.	

b. In your view, which of the four characters (Romeo, Mercutio, Benvolio and Tybalt) is most responsible for the deaths that occur? Support your answer using the quotations you have found.

Interpretations of Tybalt and Mercutio

Activity 6

As with all the characters in the play, there are different ways to interpret the characters of Tybalt and Mercutio. Traditionally, audiences have warmed to Mercutio for his exuberance and humour, whereas many have condemned Tybalt for his unflinching violence. However, you can choose an alternative interpretation.

a. Read the following interpretations and consider which is closest to your own view of Tybalt and Mercutio. Circle your choices.

> There is little to admire in the character of Tybalt; he is nothing more than a **symbol** of mindless violence.

> Mercutio is chaotic and dangerous; his volatile and immoral character is unpredictable and he causes trouble wherever he goes.

> Tybalt is highly principled and shows both courage and a strong sense of justice in his words and actions.

> It is ironic that it is Mercutio's loyalty to his friends, and to Romeo in particular, that leads not only to his own death, but to the deaths of many others too.

> Tybalt may have many fine qualities as a young man, but his bravery is undermined by his arrogance and a false sense of right and wrong.

> Mercutio is a far more exciting, energetic and engaging character than Romeo, and Shakespeare had to kill him off in Act 3 so he didn't steal the show entirely.

b. See how the following student has explained their choice of interpretation.

Tybalt has very clear principles of right and wrong, believing Romeo's appearance at the ball to be an insult to his family. He believes firmly in justice and is willing to carry out that justice bravely himself, as he does by challenging Romeo, despite the risk to himself. He is consistent and fair in his actions and is worthy of respect.

On separate paper, explain your choice of interpretation, using references to any part of the text to support your response.

Writing about Tybalt – with support

Activity 7

Here is an exam-style task focusing on the character of Tybalt. Underline and annotate the key words in the task. What precisely are you being asked to do?

> **How does Shakespeare present Tybalt as a contrast to Romeo in this extract from Act 3 Scene 1?**

Activity 8

Look at the notes on the extract from Act 3 Scene 1 below that a student has made in preparing for this task. They are a list of Tybalt's characteristics in this scene, but not all of them compare well with Romeo. Circle the three points you would choose to help answer this task.

Mercutio	Men's eyes were made to look, and let them gaze; I will not budge for no man's pleasure, I.
	Enter Romeo
Tybalt	Well, peace be with you, sir, here comes my man. *→ calm / polite*
Mercutio	But I'll be hang'd, sir, if he wear your livery. Marry, go before to field, he'll be your follower; Your worship in that sense may call him man.
Tybalt	Romeo, the love I bear thee can afford No better term than this: thou art a villain. *← single-minded*
Romeo	Tybalt, the reason that I have to love thee Doth much excuse the appertaining rage To such a greeting. Villain am I none; Therefore farewell, I see thou knowest me not.
Tybalt	Boy, this shall not excuse the injuries *← murderous* That thou hast done me, therefore turn and draw. *← determined*

Activity 9

The exam-style task in Activity 7 is focused on a contrast between Tybalt and Romeo. Read one student's argument below, and annotate to show where it has included the following ideas.

In this extract, Shakespeare creates a powerful confrontation between two key male characters: Tybalt who is calm, single-minded and murderous, and Romeo, who is full of love and goodwill, bringing together the dual ideas of death and love that run throughout the whole play.

comparison of the characteristics of Tybalt and Romeo

impact of the contrast

references to big ideas or **context.**

Activity 10

Read the following good response to the task in Activity 7 on page 53, along with the examiner's notes. The student has not made many references to the context of the play.

Use three different colours to highlight the response to show where the student could have included references to the following big ideas: masculinity, death and love.

In this extract, Shakespeare creates a powerful confrontation between two key male characters: Tybalt who is calm, single-minded and murderous, and Romeo, who is full of love and goodwill, bringing together the dual ideas of death and love that run throughout the whole play.

Tybalt and Romeo are both very calm in this scene. However, while Romeo is calm and rational, Tybalt is calm but irrational. He thinks that Romeo attending the Capulet's ball was an action that deserves to be punished by death. Tybalt addresses Romeo by name and calmly insults him: 'Romeo ... thou art a villain.' The audience knows by this point in the play that Tybalt's true character is violent and that he hates 'all Montagues', so they know what he is capable of. The calmness is unnatural and creates even greater tension as the audience waits to see Tybalt explode with rage. Tybalt's calmness contrasts with Romeo's moderate response to the insult, which is to echo the same word: 'Villain am I none.' The simplicity of the language is deliberate so as not to distract from the physical and visual drama on stage.

Tybalt is also single-minded. He is only interested in fighting Romeo and is unwilling to fight Mercutio. Romeo's entrance is one of the most powerful in the play, as the audience clearly anticipates the conflict between Tybalt and him. All the tension and action in the scene builds towards this climax. Tybalt greets Romeo with simple monosyllables, saying 'Here comes my man', again to increase the tension. This contrasts with Romeo, who has more interests than the family feud. He has friendships, a new wife and shows little interest in fighting.

Finally, Tybalt is murderous. Tybalt's morality is flawed as he sees killing others to be a suitable punishment just for them being Montagues. In Act 1 Scene 5, he says 'To strike him dead I hold it not a sin', which shows he feels death is justified by God. Romeo, on the other hand, is so in love with Juliet that he feels love for all men but Tybalt calls out 'turn and draw', which is a direct command and a threat. Romeo's action was very dangerous in the fight because it left him unprotected, but he only wants peace and harmony because he has married a Capulet and has no reason to hate Tybalt.

Shakespeare contrasts Tybalt's calm, murderous aggression with Romeo's peaceful, sensitive love for everyone. Shakespeare chooses to highlight this contrast by juxtaposing them in this scene and offering the audience an opportunity to judge for themselves which approach is morally valid.

The student opens with a direct comparison between the two characters, making a subtle and effective distinction between being rational and irrational. This is supported by references to other parts of the play, and is developed to suggest the impact this has on the audience. The student weaves some language analysis into their argument and also shows an awareness of the scene visually.

The simple structure of the argument is effective in signposting to the examiner how each point is detailed in turn. The focus on Tybalt's single-mindedness contrasted with Romeo's multiple concerns is not particularly well-developed, although the student comments on the structure of the scene well.

The student engages with the third point in their argument, that Tybalt is murderous, but does not engage in detail with ideas of masculinity as would be expected in a higher-level response. The contrast between Tybalt and Romeo is identified and supported with textual detail, but there is limited interpretation of themes or ideas here.

The final paragraph concludes by emphasising the main argument effectively, but again does not extend their response by offering an opinion on the themes of death and love.

Writing about Mercutio – try it yourself

Use what you have learned to plan and write your response to this task.
The question refers to the same extract from Act 3 Scene 1 as on page 53.

> **How does Shakespeare present Mercutio as a contrast to Romeo in this extract from Act 3 Scene 1?**

a. Now write a plan for this task. Follow the three stages below to plan your answer.

Stage 1 – Make notes and organise your ideas about:

- the characteristics of Mercutio, such as his humour

- the characteristics of Romeo, such as his seriousness

- the big ideas or themes in the extract, such as masculinity, honour

----

Stage 2 – Decide on the main argument for the introduction. Think about these questions.

- Is Mercutio presented differently here to the rest of the play? If so, how, and why?

- How are Mercutio and Romeo portrayed similarly or differently in this scene?

- What has the audience learned about Mercutio from earlier scenes that affects the way we respond to him here?

- What does Mercutio contribute to our understanding of the big ideas?

Stage 3 – Consider how to include language, structure, stagecraft and context. Annotate the extract on page 53 to highlight the methods used and their effects.

b. On separate paper, write your response to the exam-style task.

Love and hatred

Key ideas about love and hatred

1. The love between Romeo and Juliet is the heart of the play, illustrating the timeless beauty and power of romantic love.

2. There are different types of love conveyed, including the pain and pointlessness of **unrequited love**.

3. Hatred is shown to be a destructive force throughout the play and to have far-reaching consequences.

4. Love and how it is expressed within families is shown to be challenging, particularly in the relationship between Juliet and her parents.

5. **Platonic love** between friends and confidants is shown to have value alongside romantic love.

Key quotations

'O brawling love, O loving hate' (Romeo, Act 1 Scene 1)

'This bud of love' (Juliet, Act 2 Scene 2)

Juliet's view of love is fragile, natural and beautiful; the bud is full of promise, as is her new, youthful love for Romeo.

'I hate hell, all Montagues, and thee.' (Tybalt, Act 1 Scene 1)

'love-devouring Death do what he dare' (Romeo, Act 2 Scene 6)

'See what a scourge is laid upon your hate' (Prince, Act 5 Scene 3)

Key events and structure

Act 1 Scene 1
The hatred between the two families erupts in a brawl in the opening scene. Romeo's unrequited love for Rosaline, as described to Benvolio, sets up a comparison with his later love for Juliet.

Act 1 Scene 3
Lady Capulet tells Juliet about Paris's marriage proposal. Their formal relationship indicates an absence of love between Lady Capulet and Juliet.

Act 1 Scene 5
Romeo and Juliet fall in love at first sight at the Capulet party, establishing the symbolic significance of love.

Act 2 Scene 2
Romeo and Juliet confess their love to each other and agree to marry. The swift pace of their relationship reflects love's power to influence events.

Act 3 Scene 1
Romeo's love for Juliet initially leads him to refuse to fight her cousin, Tybalt. Tybalt's hatred of Romeo leads to both his and Mercutio's death, thus Tybalt is wholly identified with hatred.

Act 5 Scene 3
Romeo and Juliet choose to die rather than live without each other. Through this tragic outcome, the hatred between the Capulets and Montagues is resolved.

Exploring love and hatred
What is love?

Love is at the heart of *Romeo and Juliet*, although Shakespeare chooses to portray romantic love alongside other types of love, and against a backdrop of hatred between the two feuding families. Through the action of the play, he invites the audience to question their own attitudes to love in all its various guises.

a. Complete the spidergram below to show where the following qualities of love and hatred are shown in the play. Think about characters' actions and their relationships with others.

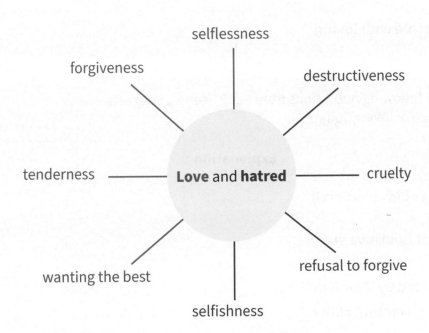

selflessness

forgiveness

destructiveness

tenderness —— **Love** and **hatred** —— cruelty

wanting the best

refusal to forgive

selfishness

b. Summarise in one sentence how you think love is portrayed in the play as a whole. Do the same for hatred.

   i. Love: ....

    ....

   ii. Hatred: ....

    ....

Unrequited love versus love at first sight

Activity 2

Shakespeare gives us an image of unrequited love, as Romeo describes the misery and despair of loving Rosaline without any hope of her returning his love. This contrasts with the idea of 'love at first sight', which is shown when Romeo and Juliet meet at the masked ball for the first time.

a. Explain what each of the following quotations from Act 1 Scene 1 suggests about Romeo's experience of loving Rosaline.

Quotation	Explanation
'This love feel I, that feel no love in this'	
'Love is a smoke made with the fume of sighs'	
'Love is … a sea nourish'd with loving tears'	

b. Explain what each of the following quotations from Act 2 Scene 2 suggests about Romeo's experience of loving Juliet.

Quotation	Explanation
'With love's light wings did I o'erperch these walls, For stony limits cannot hold love out'	
'My life were better ended by their hate, Than death prorogued, wanting of thy love.'	
'Love goes toward love as schoolboys from their books'	

c. Compare the words spoken by Romeo to describe his love for Rosaline with the words and images he uses to describe his love for Juliet. What do the differences tell us about the love he feels for Juliet?

The imagery of love and hatred

Love and hatred are both abstract concepts, so writers often turn to images to embody the ideas and help the audience to imagine the feelings.

a. For each of the quotations below, explore the effects of the language used to describe love. The first one has been done for you.

   i. **'This bud of love, by summer's ripening breath,**

      May prove a beauteous flower when next we meet.' (Juliet, Act 2 Scene 2)

> Juliet uses an image of a flower to describe her love for Romeo. The 'bud' is a symbol of the newness of their love, something which will blossom in the future.

   ii. **'How silver-sweet sound lovers' tongues by night,**

      Like softest music to attending ears!' (Romeo, Act 2 Scene 2)

   iii. **'These violent delights have violent ends,**

      And in their triumph die like fire and powder,

      Which as they kiss consume.' (Friar Lawrence, Act 2 Scene 6)

b. For each of the quotations below, explore the effects of the language used to describe hatred.

   i. **'What ho, you men, you beasts!**

      That quench the fire of your pernicious rage

      With purple fountains issuing from your veins' (Prince, Act 1 Scene 1)

   ii. **'to part your canker'd hate'** (Prince, Act 1 Scene 1)

   iii. **'but this intrusion shall,**

      Now seeming sweet, convert to bitt'rest gall.' (Tybalt, Act 1 Scene 5)

Structure and stagecraft

Activity 4

Shakespeare structures the play to present the dominant theme of love against the background of the hatred that exists between the two families.

a. Why does Shakespeare alternate scenes of love with scenes of hatred throughout the play? What effects does this create?

----

b. How does Shakespeare dramatise the theme of hatred in the play? Think about the use of **imagery**, symbolism and stage props such as swords, as well as the ways conflict between characters is presented.

Activity 5

There are plenty of examples of **platonic love** in the play, such as the friendships and strong family relationships. However, these relationships suffer setbacks as the dramatic events take place.

a. Complete the table below to identify how each of these relationships suffers and why.

Relationship	How it went wrong	Why love failed
Nurse's love for Juliet – nurse and confidante	Betrayed Juliet by advising her to abandon Romeo	Misjudged Juliet's feelings for Romeo
Friar Lawrence's love for Romeo		
Romeo's love for Mercutio		
Lady Capulet's love for Juliet		
Lord Capulet's love for Juliet		

b. Choose one of these relationships. Explain in more detail on separate paper how and why love failed the test of events.

Writing about love and hatred – with support

Here is an exam-style task focusing on the themes of love and hatred. Underline and annotate the key words and phrases in the task. What precisely are you being asked to do?

> **How does Shakespeare convey the power of love in this extract from Act 2 Scene 2?**

Read the extract below from Act 2 Scene 2.

a. Make notes on the extract to show where Shakespeare has referred to the power of love; used imagery to explain the power of love, and used structure or **stagecraft** to enhance the power of love.

Juliet	What man art thou that thus bescreen'd in night So stumblest on my counsel?
Romeo	By a name I know not how to tell thee who I am. My name, dear saint, is hateful to myself, Because it is an enemy to thee; Had I it written, I would tear the word.
Juliet	My ears have yet not drunk a hundred words Of thy tongue's uttering, yet I know the sound. Art thou not Romeo, and a Montague?
Romeo	Neither, fair maid, if either thee dislike.
Juliet	How cam'st thou hither, tell me, and wherefore? The orchard walls are high and hard to climb, And the place death, considering who thou art, If any of my kinsmen find thee here.
Romeo	With love's light wings did I o'erperch these walls, For stony limits cannot hold love out, And what love can do, that dares love attempt: Therefore thy kinsmen are no stop to me.

b. Read the following statements about the power of love and consider which you think best fits the question and the extract. Circle your choice.

> Shakespeare demonstrates how love fools people into believing that they can overcome any obstacle, but the moral rules of a conservative, religious society like Verona will always win.

> Shakespeare conveys that love can overcome hatred, conflict, loyalty to family and parental bonds, but death will always triumph in the end.

> Shakespeare wanted to show in the play how love is so powerful it can conquer all, including death.

Activity 8

Read the following excellent response to the task in Activity 6.

Use four different colours to highlight where the student has successfully commented on:

a. the power of love and any other big ideas

b. language

c. structure

d. stagecraft

In *Romeo and Juliet*, Shakespeare conveys that love can overcome hatred, conflict, loyalty to family and parental bonds, but death will always triumph in the end. The extract shows how Romeo and Juliet feel all-powerful, but it is only an illusion because, as the audience know from the Chorus at the start, it is a story of 'death-marked love'. Shakespeare exploits the dramatic irony to reinforce the inevitability of their doomed love.

Shakespeare shows the power of love in very visual ways, by having Romeo climb the orchard walls to see Juliet again after the party. Juliet says the walls are high and hard to climb, but love gives Romeo the strength and courage to brave the kinsmen who would kill him if they found him there. Romeo's confidence is shown in the line 'And what love can do, that dares love attempt', personifying love as a daring adventurer, just like himself. He is full to the brim with the power of love.

Romeo describes 'love's light wings' as if love is a bird or supernatural being that can magically lift him over the 'stony limits' he faces. The soft, airy alliteration highlights the ethereal nature of love's power to defy gravity. There are many images of light in this scene, with references to angels, stars and the moon. These all remind the audience that this scene is 'bescreen'd in night'. The darkness symbolises the dark hatred of the family feud and the light symbolises their love. There are gender stereotypes here, with Romeo being the action man and Juliet the passive female, waiting to be claimed. This is reinforced by the names Romeo calls her – 'fair maid' and 'dear saint'. However, the rest of the play dispels that idea, with Juliet showing the power of love to transform her modesty and obedience into independence and self-belief.

Both Romeo and Juliet believe that their love is powerful enough to overcome their biggest obstacle, which is their families' feud. Romeo uses an image to describe how 'hateful' his own identity as a Montague is, showing both sides of love and hate. He says he would 'tear the word' and destroy it, suggesting his identity is nothing more than a word on a piece of paper and therefore easy to overcome.

Overall, Shakespeare illustrates in this scene how powerful love is, but warns the audience with the reminder that this place is 'death'. Death is never far away in the play, and it makes a mockery of Romeo's conviction that 'stony limits cannot hold love out'. They may have got away with it this time, but death will win in the end.

Writing about love and hatred – try it yourself

Activity 9

Use what you have learned about structuring and planning an answer by writing an essay in response to the following exam-style task.

> **How does Shakespeare present ideas of love and hate in the play as a whole?**

a. Before you start to plan your answer, consider these questions:

- What is the effect of the **contrast** between love and hatred?
- How does Shakespeare interweave these two ideas?
- Which does Shakespeare believe is the more powerful?
- Which triumphs in the end?

b. Summarise your response to the essay task in one sentence and use this as your main argument.

----

c. Plan your answer on separate paper. You could note down on your plan:

- the imagery Shakespeare uses to describe love and hate
- the way Shakespeare structures the play to focus on the two contrasting ideas
- the way Shakespeare identifies specific characters to **symbolise** love and hatred
- the different visual effects involved in staging scenes that deal predominantly with love and hate.

d. Start writing your answer below and complete your essay on separate paper.

Peace and conflict

Key ideas about peace and conflict

1. The opening Prologue explains the conflict that drives the drama of the play.

2. There are different types of conflict within the play – psychological, emotional, physical, moral and religious.

3. All characters are involved in the conflict. It spans generations and social classes.

4. Some characters act as peacemakers, while others **symbolise** violence and conflict.

5. Most of Shakespeare's plays end with peace restored, but in *Romeo and Juliet,* peace is marked by the tragic outcome.

Key quotations

> **'What, drawn and talk of peace? I hate the word'** (Tybalt, Act 1 Scene 1)

This mocking rhetorical question in the opening scene introduces the idea of peace and marks out Tybalt as hostile to the idea.

'These violent delights have violent ends' (Friar Lawrence, Act 2 Scene 6)

'Gentle Mercutio, put thy rapier up' (Romeo, Act 3 Scene 1)

'For now, these hot days, is the mad blood stirring' (Benvolio, Act 3 Scene 1)

'A glooming peace this morning with it brings' (Prince, Act 5 Scene 3)

Key events and structure

Act 1 Scene 1
The play opens with leading members of two warring families fighting on the street and the 'ancient grudge' is introduced by the Chorus in the Prologue.

Act 1 Scene 5
The masked ball alternates between peace and conflict, as Romeo and Juliet's meeting and first kiss takes place against the backdrop of Tybalt's threat of violence.

Act 2 Scene 6
Romeo and Juliet are married at Friar Lawrence's cell. This peaceful scene has a slower pace but **foreshadows** future conflict too.

Act 3 Scene 1
There is violent conflict on the streets as Mercutio, Tybalt and Romeo fight. Initially a peacemaker, Romeo's actions lead to Mercutio's death, and he kills Tybalt in revenge.

Act 3 Scene 5
The initial peace of Romeo and Juliet's wedding night turns to domestic conflict in the Capulet family, creating dramatic **contrast**.

Act 5 Scene 3
Conflict breaks out at the Capulet tomb, but all is peaceful in death and the two families form a truce.

Exploring peace and conflict
Peace as passive

Peace is essentially a passive state, whereas conflict is active, dynamic and exciting. All drama is founded on conflict. Not all conflict is violent, but Shakespeare chooses to dramatise the various conflicts in the play by bringing them alive visually and often violently.

Complete the table below to show the various conflicts in the play and whether they are resolved or not by the end of the play. The first one has been done for you.

Type of conflict	Example and characters involved	Resolution
emotional	The Nurse tries to persuade Juliet to marry Paris and forget about Romeo.	It is unresolved as Juliet never explains her feelings of betrayal.
social		
psychological		
violent		
domestic		
legal		

Ancient grudge to new mutiny

Activity 2

a. Read the Prince's speech from Act 1 Scene 1 where he stops the fighting between the Capulets and Montagues. Annotate the extract to identify references to peace and conflict, and the language techniques used to convey these.

> Rebellious subjects, enemies to peace,
>
> Profaners of this neighbour-stained steel—
>
> Will they not hear?—What ho, you men, you beasts!
>
> That quench the fire of your pernicious rage
>
> With purple fountains issuing from your veins:
>
> On pain of torture, from those bloody hands ←——— *Shakespeare introduces blood as a symbol of the conflict that pervades every scene and every aspect of the play.*
>
> Throw your mistemper'd weapons to the ground,
>
> And hear the sentence of your moved prince.
>
> Three civil brawls, bred of an airy word,
>
> By thee, old Capulet, and Montague,
>
> Have thrice disturb'd the quiet of our streets,

b. Summarise the Prince's attitude to the conflict between the two families.

Activity 3

Alongside the physical conflict, the play also explores inner conflict in the characters. One example is when Juliet finds out Romeo killed Tybalt. Analyse the effect of the language used in the following quotations from Juliet to describe her inner conflict in Act 3 Scene 2. The first has been done for you.

a. **'O serpent heart, hid with a flow'ring face!'**

> The serpent reminds us of the bible story of the devil seducing Eve, suggesting Romeo has deceitfully drawn Juliet into a relationship, while the word 'heart' links the serpent with romance. The 'flow'ring face' extends the metaphor, creating the idea that the devil appears beautiful, like a flower, which hides the ugliness of the serpent. Juliet is struggling to cope with the conflict of good and evil in someone she has idealised.

b. **'Dove-feather'd raven, wolvish-ravening lamb!'**

----

c. **'Was ever book containing such vile matter
   So fairly bound?'**

> **Tip**
>
> The metaphor of a book is also used earlier in the play when Lady Capulet describes Paris to Juliet in Act 1 Scene 3. In an essay response, it is useful to compare the link between two similar metaphors from different parts of the play, and compare how they are used and the links between them.

Family conflict

Activity 4

One of the most compelling scenes in the play is the confrontation between Juliet and her parents in Act 3 Scene 5. How far this becomes a physical conflict depends on the director of the play, but many audiences have found this scene to be a display of cruel conflict between the generations.

a. Why do you think Shakespeare opens this scene with the peaceful waking of Romeo and Juliet after their wedding night?

b. Why do you think Shakespeare introduces Lady Capulet first, before bringing Lord Capulet into the scene? How does this build the conflict in the scene?

c. How does the dialogue echo the conflict of the scene?

d. How does the presence of the Nurse contribute to the drama of the scene? Do her contributions increase or decrease the tension?

e. What evidence can you find in Shakespeare's language that he intended the conflict between Lord Capulet and Juliet to be physical? Explain your answer.

Conflict on the streets

In the first scene of the play, the Prince rebukes Lord Capulet and Lord Montague for being 'enemies to peace' and threatening the state of Verona with their 'ancient quarrel'. In the final scene, the Prince deplores the terrible tragedy that has brought the two families to realise the folly of their feud, and he brokers a despairing peace between the two old men. Peace has come – but at a very high price.

a. Read and annotate this short extract from the Prince's final speech in Act 5 Scene 3 to explore his point of view on the conflict.

> Where be these enemies? Capulet, Montague?
>
> See what a scourge is laid upon your hate,
>
> That heaven finds means to kill your joys with love!
>
> And I for winking at your discords too
>
> Have lost a brace of kinsmen. All are punish'd.

The Prince clearly blames the two men for their actions and attitude.

b. Use what you have learned to decide which of the following statements best represents Shakespeare's perspective in the play. Circle your chosen statement, and explain your choice below with reference to the play.

- Conflict will always end in tragedy.

- Peace is something we should strive to achieve, but it comes at a price.

- Peace and conflict are necessary for any progress to be made in life.

Tip

Themes often come in pairs. They are often opposites, each one reinforcing and highlighting the other, eternally linked. For example, Tybalt's great love for his family is the cause of his hatred for the Montagues.

Writing about peace and conflict – with support

Activity 6

Here is an exam-style task focusing on the theme of peace. Underline and annotate the key words and phrases in the task. What precisely is it asking you to do?

> **How does Shakespeare present the importance of peace in the play as a whole?**

Activity 7

The task focuses not just on peace, but on the importance of peace. This means you will need to make a judgement about how far peace is important to the play.

a. Read the following statements about the importance of peace in the play. Circle the one that you think best fits the question.

> Peace is an important motivation for some characters but not all; others seem to thrive on conflict.

> Peace is not very important in the play; it is conflict that is more exciting and dramatic.

> Peace is important, but Shakespeare shows that you can't have peace without conflict; the play is all about the need for opposites.

b. Look at this student's plan for the task in Activity 6. On separate paper, make your own plan to support one of the other statements above.

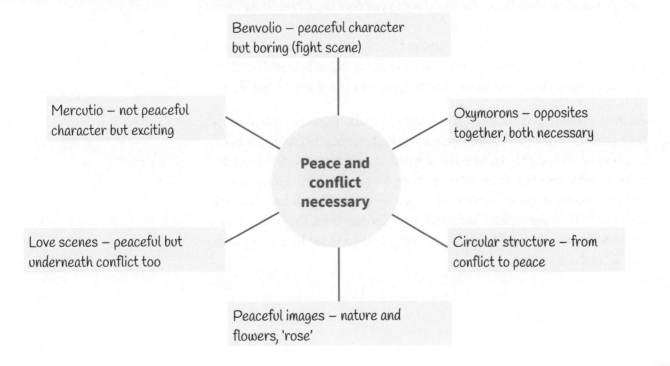

Benvolio – peaceful character but boring (fight scene)

Mercutio – not peaceful character but exciting

Oxymorons – opposites together, both necessary

Peace and conflict necessary

Love scenes – peaceful but underneath conflict too

Circular structure – from conflict to peace

Peaceful images – nature and flowers, 'rose'

Activity 8

Read the following excellent response to the task in Activity 6, along with the examiner's notes. Add your own comments to show where you think the student has done well to address the task.

EXCELLENT

Peace is important, but Shakespeare shows that you can't have peace without conflict; the play is all about the need for opposites. Many of the characters are motivated by the desire for a peaceful life, but some of the most interesting characters are those who are motivated by the desire for conflict.

Benvolio is one of the characters who is always seeking peace. In the opening scene, he tries to stop the fighting between the Capulets and the Montagues, and even tries to persuade Tybalt to help him calm the situation. 'I do but keep the peace' Benvolio says, showing in his simple language that he has a simple aim. The same is shown in Act 3 Scene 1, where he tells Mercutio to retire as the day is hot and 'the mad blood' is stirring, hinting at violent conflict as something crazy. Benvolio, whose name means 'good will' is almost too angelic. Mercutio, who stirs up trouble and is the cause of much of the tragedy in the play, is a far more attractive character. The audience is on his side, willing him to challenge Tybalt, not listen to meek and mild Benvolio. So while peace is important, conflict is more exciting.

← The student focuses on the most obviously peaceful character, Benvolio, with correct quotations to support their point. This point is developed by contrasting with Mercutio's anger and the impact on the audience.

Romeo and Juliet's love scenes are mostly peaceful, which reinforces the importance of peace. The balcony scene in particular is slower in pace and more gentle in mood than the scenes of conflict. Shakespeare lingers over these scenes, playing with the dialogue, which goes back and forth between the lovers and elaborates on the imagery they use to describe their love. Juliet describes her 'bounty' as being as 'boundless as the sea' as they both draw on peaceful natural images, such as the ocean and stars to compare their love. These images of infinite water and space are beautiful and peaceful, but it is not their love that ultimately heals the conflict but their violent deaths. Shakespeare uses a circular structure to show the journey from conflict to peace, but in between he mixes scenes of conflict and more peaceful scenes, just like the drama of real life.

As the Chorus says at the start, it is only their 'death-mark'd love' that causes their parents' rage to end. Shakespeare deliberately uses opposites all the way through the play to show how both are necessary parts of life. He uses oxymorons to bring these two sides together, for example 'O brawling love' and 'an honourable villain.' These vivid images are unexpected and challenge the audience to think about peace and conflict in their own lives. Peace is certainly important in the play, but Shakespeare is clear that you can't have peace without conflict and vice versa.

Writing about peace and conflict – try it yourself

Use what you have learned about structuring and planning your response to practise writing about peace and conflict. Underline and annotate the key words in the exam question below. What precisely are you being asked to do?

> **Discuss how Shakespeare explores the theme of conflict in the play as a whole.**

a. To help you plan your answer, make notes about:

- where conflict appears in the play, choosing specific scenes

- the different types of conflict, selecting a variety

- how conflict is presented, visually, dramatically and linguistically in different scenes.

----

b. Summarise your response to the essay task in one sentence and use this as your main argument. Think about the following questions to help you develop your ideas.

- What is Shakespeare's purpose in creating conflict between characters?

- How and why is conflict resolved?

----

c. Start writing your answer below and complete your essay on separate paper. For each point you make, ensure there is an opportunity for you to comment on the language, structure or **stagecraft** Shakespeare uses to convey that point.

Youth and age

Key ideas about youth and age

1. Romeo and Juliet are youthful **protagonists**. At times impetuous, both characters also display maturity beyond their years.

2. The action of the play explicitly sets young and old against each other, such as conflict between Juliet and her parents.

3. Some characters conform to age stereotypes, but all bear the moral responsibility of their age and time of life.

4. Shakespeare invites the audience to appreciate the vibrancy of youth, although age often represents power in the play.

5. The young and the old are both essential to the cycle of life, which adds to the tragedy at the end of young lives sacrificed.

Key quotations

''tis not hard, I think,
For men so old as we to keep the peace.'
(Lord Capulet, Act 1 Scene 2)

'Had she affections and warm youthful blood' (Juliet, Act 2 Scene 5)

'Now old desire doth in his death-bed lie,
And young affection gapes to be his heir' (Chorus, Act 1 Scene 5)

Age and youth are personified to bring these abstract ideas alive, almost like characters in the play.

'Wert thou as young as I …'
(Romeo, Act 3 Scene 3)

'let my old life
Be sacrific'd'
(Friar Lawrence, Act 5 Scene 3)

Key events and structure

Act 1 Scene 1
The young servants begin the fighting, followed by the older members of the families; conflict is established across all age groups.

Act 1 Scenes 2 and 3
At first, Lord Capulet refuses Paris's request to marry Juliet, saying she is too young, but in conversation with the Nurse, Lady Capulet encourages Juliet to consider Paris's proposal, having been married at a similarly young age herself.

Act 1 Scene 5
Lord Capulet rebukes his young kinsman, Tybalt, at the ball; the contrast between their attitudes highlights their age difference.

Act 2 Scenes 3, 4, 5 and 6
Romeo and Juliet seek the support of Friar Lawrence and the Nurse as their mutual love accelerates to marriage.

Act 3 Scenes 2 and 3
The Nurse and Friar Lawrence comfort and advise the young lovers in their distress; both sets of characters are defined in these scenes by their ages and their roles.

Act 5 Scene 3
In the Capulets' tomb, the older generation mourn the deaths of five young people as the play ends with a lost generation.

Exploring youth and age
Age stereotypes

Activity 1

The theme of youth and age is slightly different to other themes: while characters are shown to behave in different ways in the play, such as violently or treacherously or peacefully, their age is just a fact. We are all defined by our age to some extent, and the characters in the play are no different. Society can have expectations of how characters will speak and act, depending on their time of life. Shakespeare often uses these stereotypes but occasionally chooses to develop characters in unexpected ways. This is done for humorous effect in places but also for more serious purposes.

a. Read the list of characteristics below. Add the characteristics that you think are stereotypical of the older and younger generations to the table.

powerful   vibrant   forward looking   innovative   respectful   impulsive

authoritarian   wise   powerless   dull   traditional   disrespectful

foolish   cautious   rebellious   backward looking

The younger generation	The older generation

b. Add the name, in brackets, of any character in the play whom you feel demonstrates a particular **characteristic**.

c. How far do you think the characters in the play conform to these stereotypes?

The benefits of age

There are a number of characters whose age Shakespeare doesn't make clear, but the main older characters are the lords Capulet and Montague, the Nurse and Friar Lawrence. They represent Shakespeare's perspective on the value of age, wisdom and experience.

a. How does Shakespeare present Lord Montague and Lord Capulet in the first scene?

---

b. Why do you think he chose to mock them in this way?

---

c. How does Shakespeare establish the Nurse's age in Act 1 Scene 3?

---

d. What impression does this give the audience of her maturity and judgement?

---

e. What impression are we given of the relationship between Lord and Lady Capulet, given that he is described as an old man and she cannot be much older than 26 years?

---

f. How does Shakespeare present Friar Lawrence's age in a positive light in Act 2 Scene 3?

The generation gap

The generation gap is most vividly exposed in the relationship between Lord Capulet and Juliet.

Analyse the attitudes expressed in each of the following quotations, and comment on the language used, where appropriate. The first one has been done for you.

Lord Capulet quotation	Analysis
'I think she will be rul'd In all respects by me' (Act 3 Scene 4)	In Act 1, Lord Capulet tells Paris that he will allow Juliet some say in who she marries. However, as circumstances change, he states: 'I think she will be rul'd / In all respects by me', showing he expects Juliet's complete obedience. This hardening of his approach is reinforced by direct confrontation between parents and daughter.
'Have you deliver'd to her our decree?' (Act 3 Scene 5)	
'Hang thee, young baggage, disobedient wretch!' (Act 3 Scene 5)	

Juliet quotation	Analysis
'Good father, I beseech you on my knees' (Act 3 Scene 5)	
'O sweet my mother, cast me not away!' (Act 3 Scene 5)	
'I pray you tell my lord and father, madam, I will not marry yet' (Act 3 Scene 5)	

Interpretations of youth and age

The play is not alone in dealing with the challenges of the generation divide and exploring the confrontations that ensue. Traditional narratives involving conflict between generations often end with the young learning the lessons of their foolish, youthful ambitions, and the older generation reluctantly but generously handing over their power. This is very different to the narrative journey in *Romeo and Juliet*, where the play ends with a generation of passionate, mature young people lying dead in a tomb, and an embittered, weary older generation agreeing a gloomy truce.

a. Which of the following statements best fits your understanding of Shakespeare's views on youth and age? Circle your choice.

Shakespeare's play begins with a comic portrayal of age but ends tragically with the failure of the older generation to understand the younger generation.

Romeo and Juliet **symbolise** many of the positive qualities of the young, for example their passion and their rebellion against the authority of their elders; the tragedy is that this ends in their deaths. It is Shakespeare's warning to us all to value the young.

Age is associated with a responsible use of power and the wise management of people; the older characters in the play fail in their duty of care towards the young people in the play, and pay a huge price for their failure.

b. Look at how the following student has explained their choice.

The first scene includes old men fighting in their nightgowns, which shows Shakespeare making fun of them, but Lord Capulet especially makes life very difficult for the younger people. The end shows how the older characters have ruined the lives of the young people, without really meaning to.

Explain your choice of statement, using examples from the play to support your view.

Writing about youth and age – with support

Activity 5

Here is an exam-style task focusing on the theme of youth. Underline and annotate the key words and phrases in the task. What precisely are you being asked to do?

> **How does Shakespeare present youth in this extract from Act 2 Scene 5 and in the play as a whole?**

Juliet   The clock struck nine when I did send the Nurse; ← *Juliet is impatient.*
          In half an hour she promis'd to return.
          Perchance she cannot meet him: that's not so.
          O, she is lame! Love's heralds should be thoughts,
          Which ten times faster glides than the sun's beams,
          Driving back shadows over low'ring hills;
          Therefore do nimble-pinion'd doves draw Love,
          And therefore hath the wind-swift Cupid wings.
          Now is the sun upon the highmost hill
          Of this day's journey, and from nine till twelve
          Is three long hours, yet she is not come.
          Had she affections and warm youthful blood,
          She would be as swift in motion as a ball;
          My words would bandy her to my sweet love,
          And his to me.
          But old folks, many feign as they were dead,
          Unwieldy, slow, heavy, and pale as lead.
          Enter Nurse *with* Peter
          O God, she comes! O honey Nurse, what news?

Activity 6

a. Annotate the extract to show the typical features of youth demonstrated by Juliet in this speech. One annotation has been added for you.

b. Annotate the extract to identify and comment on the effects of the following methods:

- **soliloquy**
- **hyperbole**
- **foreshadowing**
- fanciful **imagery**
- **stagecraft**, such as the Nurse's entrance
- **mood**/pace.

Activity 7

Read this excellent response to the exam-style task in Activity 5, along with the examiner's notes. Use four different colours to highlight where the student has:

a. set out their main argument

b. referred to key ideas and themes

c. commented on the methods used

d. included textual references to support their points.

EXCELLENT

Shakespeare wants the audience to engage closely with the younger characters as ← they develop over the course of the play. Juliet is not perfect, but she shows such maturity that it is truly tragic to witness her young life ended by the failures of the older generation. Shakespeare celebrates youth and mourns its death.

The student sets out their main argument in the opening paragraph and includes context from the essay task, linking their argument to the theme of youth, and bringing in another big idea from the play – death.

In the extract, Juliet comes across as impatient, saying 'from nine till twelve is three long hours' and 'Love's heralds should be thoughts, which ten times faster glides than the sun's beams'. Juliet reveals a childish pleasure in these statistics. She repeats the time 'the clock struck nine' to remind the audience of the passing of time, which is important in live performance as time can pass differently.

←

The student identifies two typical features of youth: impatience and a childish pleasure in times. These are supported by textual references and comments on literary methods used.

She is obsessed with love, as is typical of people her age, and she uses romantic imagery to reflect this: 'therefore hath the wind-swift Cupid wings', drawing on images of conventional love mythology, and again emphasising the passing of time. Her romantic fantasy and overdramatic impatience are expressed in this extract in a soliloquy, which invites the audience to share the intimacy and innocence of her youthful desire.

Juliet complains about the Nurse's age, using a childlike simile: 'Had she affections and warm youthful blood/She would be as swift in motion as a ball'. The implication is that Juliet has all these 'youthful' characteristics. When the Nurse enters, the pace and the mood of the scene changes from one of slow frustration to fast, excited anticipation: 'O honey Nurse, what news?' The endearing term 'honey' reinforces Juliet's sweetness and kindness – positive qualities of the young.

Shakespeare includes another reference to age, contrasting youth and age as he does many of his themes to highlight their differences. But this reference foreshadows Juliet's death: 'But old folks, many feign as they were dead, / Unwieldy, slow, heavy, and pale as lead.' In this image, Shakespeare reminds us of the dark background to the play, and the tragic ending, which intensifies the sense of Juliet's youth and joy.

By the end of the play, Juliet has matured into an independent, confident, free-thinking woman. The audience has shared her journey, as she deals with the death of her cousin, the betrayal of her Nurse, the threats of her parents, and the exile of her husband. Shakespeare contrasts her youthful good sense and judgement with the cruelty of her parents, the disloyalty of her Nurse, the careless planning of the Friar and the pointless feud started by the older generation. The audience is invited to empathise and identify with the youth in the play more powerfully than with the older characters.

Writing about youth and age – try it yourself

Use what you have learned to plan and write your response to this exam-style task.

> **Discuss how Shakespeare presents the conflict between youth and age in this extract from Act 1 Scene 5 and in the play as a whole.**

Lord Capulet	Why, how now, kinsman, wherefore storm you so?
Tybalt	Uncle, this is a Montague, our foe: A villain that is hither come in spite, To scorn at our solemnity this night.
Lord Capulet	Young Romeo is it?
Tybalt	'Tis he, that villain Romeo.
Lord Capulet	Content thee, gentle coz, let him alone, 'A bears him like a portly gentleman; And to say truth, Verona brags of him To be a virtuous and well-govern'd youth. I would not for the wealth of all this town Here in my house do him disparagement; Therefore be patient, take no note of him; It is my will, the which if thou respect, Show a fair presence, and put off these frowns, An ill-beseeming semblance for a feast.
Tybalt	It fits when such a villain is a guest: I'll not endure him.
Lord Capulet	He shall be endur'd. What, goodman boy, I say he shall, go to! Am I the master here, or you? go to! You'll not endure him? God shall mend my soul, You'll make a mutiny among my guests! You will set cock-a-hoop! you'll be the man!

Use different colours to highlight the extract to show where Shakespeare demonstrates contrasting attitudes of the youthful Tybalt and the older Lord Capulet.

On separate paper, write your response to the task in Activity 8. You should aim to write around 500 words.

Loyalty and betrayal

Key ideas about loyalty and betrayal

1. In *Romeo and Juliet*, Shakespeare explores both loyalty and betrayal, often linking them together for emphasis.

2. Loyalty can be to a person, a group, an organisation, a place or a belief. At times in the play, both **protagonists** have divided loyalties.

3. All characters in the play are loyal to someone or something; almost every character betrays someone or something too.

4. Loyalty and betrayal are closely linked in the play to ideas of honour and dishonour, honesty and deceit.

5. Romeo and Juliet question the value of their loyalty to their families and friends.

Key quotations

'O calm, dishonourable, vile submission!'
(Mercutio, Act 3 Scene 1)

'I have been feasting with mine enemy'
(Romeo, Act 2 Scene 3)

'O serpent heart, hid with a flow'ring face!'
(Juliet, Act 3 Scene 2)

Juliet struggles with divided loyalties, unable to believe her new husband can be responsible for the death of her cousin.

'Deny thy father and refuse thy name' (Juliet, Act 2 Scene 2)

'And all my fortunes at thy foot I'll lay,
And follow thee my lord throughout the world.'
(Juliet, Act 2 Scene 2)

Key events and structure

Act 1 Scene 1
The Capulets and Montagues display their family loyalty in fighting each other, establishing its importance and influence on the play from the start.

Act 1 Scene 3
In this scene, the Nurse expresses loyalty to the Capulets, and Juliet in particular, which contrasts with her betrayal later in the play.

Act 1 Scene 5
In his fiery reaction to Romeo's presence at the masked ball, Tybalt displays family loyalty and feels Lord Capulet betrays that loyalty.

Act 3 Scene 1
Tybalt is loyal to the principle of justice; Mercutio is confused by Romeo's 'dishonourable' refusal to fight; Romeo is loyal to his friend in avenging his death.

Act 3 Scene 2
When Juliet learns of Romeo's role in Tybalt's death, she struggles with conflicting loyalties to her cousin and to her husband.

Act 5 Scene 3
In this climactic scene, many characters are forced to reconcile their loyalties with the fatal consequences.

Exploring loyalty and betrayal
What is loyalty?

Activity 1

There are many examples of loyalty in the play, where characters show their devotion and commitment to a person, a group or a belief.

a. For each of the following characters in the table, identify what sort of loyalty they demonstrate. Think about to whom or to what they show their loyalty. One has been done for you.

Juliet	
Nurse	
Benvolio	Benvolio is loyal to his friends. He tries to help Romeo through his depression and encourages Mercutio to avoid fighting on the street. He is also loyal to the truth and takes responsibility for telling the Prince what has happened after the deaths of Tybalt and Mercutio.
Tybalt	
Prince	

b. Write a single sentence to summarise what you think loyalty means in the **context** of the play.

Divided loyalties

Activity 2

One of the problems with loyalty is that someone can be loyal to more than one person or group, and this can cause conflict. In *Romeo and Juliet*, Shakespeare deliberately develops the narrative to challenge the characters' loyalties. For example, at the masked ball scene in Act 1 Scene 5, Tybalt recognises Romeo and feels his family honour is questioned.

a. What does each of the following quotations from Act 1 Scene 5 tell us about the loyalties of Tybalt and Lord Capulet, and how they are divided?

   i. 'Now by the stock and honour of my kin,
      To strike him dead I hold it not a sin.' (Tybalt)

----

   ii. 'Uncle, this is a Montague, our foe:
       A villain that is hither come in spite' (Tybalt)

----

   iii. 'Content thee, gentle coz, let him alone,
        'A bears him like a portly gentleman' (Lord Capulet)

----

   iv. 'I would not for the wealth of all this town
        Here in my house do him disparagement' (Lord Capulet)

----

b. What does this scene tell us about the strength of Tybalt's loyalty?

----

c. How does Lord Capulet balance one loyalty with another?

Family loyalty

Activity 3

Loyalty to family is clearly a strong motivation for Tybalt's actions and is deeply embedded in the minds of the characters. However, it is the youngest characters, Romeo and Juliet, who dare to question this loyalty, as shown by Juliet's **soliloquy** from the balcony in Act 2 Scene 2.

a. Annotate Juliet's speech below to show:

- how Juliet questions her loyalty to family

- how the characters make sense of being supposedly enemies

- where Shakespeare explores abstract ideas such as identity

- how Shakespeare uses **imagery** of flowers and the body.

Some annotations have been added to get you started.

Juliet ready to disown her family for love

identity not about names but people

not Romeo himself who is enemy

questions which body part makes him Montague

Juliet	O Romeo, Romeo, wherefore art thou Romeo?
	Deny thy father and refuse thy name;
	Or if thou wilt not, be but sworn my love,
	And I'll no longer be a Capulet.
Romeo	*[Aside]* Shall I hear more, or shall I speak at this?
Juliet	'Tis but thy name that is my enemy;
	Thou art thyself, though not a Montague.
	What's Montague? It is nor hand nor foot,
	Nor arm nor face, nor any other part
	Belonging to a man. O be some other name!
	What's in a name? That which we call a rose
	By any other word would smell as sweet;
	So Romeo would, were he not Romeo call'd,
	Retain that dear perfection which he owes
	Without that title. Romeo, doff thy name,
	And for thy name, which is no part of thee,
	Take all myself.
Romeo	I take thee at thy word:
	Call me but love, and I'll be new baptis'd;
	Henceforth I never will be Romeo.

b. Why is this exchange between the young couple so important for their relationship as it progresses?

The betrayal of Friar Lawrence

One character in particular shows great loyalty to his young friends, to happiness and peace between the Capulet and Montague families, and to his religious beliefs. However, Friar Lawrence betrays all of them as the play progresses.

Explain how the Friar betrays one other character and what it tells us about his own character.

Interpretations of loyalty and betrayal

Like many of the other themes in the play, loyalty and betrayal appear at first to be morally clear: loyalty is good and betrayal is bad. However, Shakespeare goes some way to challenge those moral certainties and through the action of the play, asks questions about just how good loyalty is when taken too far.

a. Read the following interpretations about the presentation of the themes of loyalty and betrayal in the play. Circle the one which you think is closest to Shakespeare's view in *Romeo and Juliet*.

> Shakespeare suggests that loyalty is not always a good thing; blind loyalty can lead to a betrayal of common sense.

> Loyalty to anyone or anything, according to Shakespeare, must always be questioned and prioritised in order to avoid divided loyalties.

> Shakespeare condemns those in the play who fail in their loyalty, and he punishes those characters who betray others. He is completely in favour of loyalty.

b. Explain your choice of statement. Refer to relevant evidence from the play to support your choice.

Writing about loyalty and betrayal – with support

Here is an exam-style task focusing on themes of loyalty and betrayal that provides you with an extract from the play to write about. Underline and annotate the key words or phrases in the task. What precisely is it asking you to do?

> **How does Shakespeare convey the importance of loyalty in this extract from Act 3 Scene 5 and in the play as a whole?**

Juliet	Comfort me, counsel me.
	Alack, alack, that heaven should practise stratagems
	Upon so soft a subject as myself!
	What say'st thou? hast thou not a word of joy?
	Some comfort, Nurse.
Nurse	Faith, here it is:
	Romeo is banish'd, and all the world to nothing
	That he dares ne'er come back to challenge you;
	Or if he do, it needs must be by stealth.
	Then since the case so stands as now it doth,
	I think it best you married with the County.
	O, he's a lovely gentleman!
	Romeo's a dishclout to him. An eagle, madam,
	Hath not so green, so quick, so fair an eye
	As Paris hath. Beshrew my very heart,
	I think you are happy in this second match,
	For it excels your first, or if it did not,
	Your first is dead, or 'twere as good he were
	As living here and you no use of him.
Juliet	Speak'st thou from thy heart?
Nurse	And from my soul too, else beshrew them both.
Juliet	Amen.

Activity 7

a. Make notes on the extract to identify:

- how distressed Juliet is
- how the Nurse betrays Juliet
- how Juliet responds.

b. Read the three statements in Activity 5 on page 84 and decide which works best in response to this task.

Activity 8

Read this answer to the exam-style task in Activity 6. Using your knowledge and understanding of what makes a good essay, make comments at the end of each paragraph to identify what the student has failed to do and how they could improve their answer. The first one has been done for you.

NEEDS WORK

In this extract, Juliet is talking to the Nurse about what she should do. She is really upset because she is being forced by her parents to marry Paris, and she can't because she is already married to Romeo and that would be wrong and unfair. You can tell she is upset because she says 'Comfort me, counsel me', which shows she needs her. The Nurse has been really supportive in the past, like when Juliet needed her to arrange getting married to Romeo. She has been her Nurse since she was a baby, so she knows her really well and is very loyal.

← The student shows that the Nurse is loyal and uses a quotation to support their point — but there is no further comment to explain the language or structure. Literary terms, such as alliteration, are not included. The vocabulary is basic, and there is limited interpretation of the characters. There are no big ideas.

It is quite a big surprise when the Nurse tells Juliet she should marry Paris after all, because she was helping Juliet to marry Romeo not long ago, and now she's changed her mind. That makes it a shock, and it's why Juliet is so upset, because she expects her to help. This is because of the structure of where this scene comes in the play. She says 'Hast thou not a word of joy?', which shows she wants the Nurse to cheer her up. She expects her to be still loyal now, but she says 'I think it best you married with the County', which is not very loyal.

In this extract, the Nurse says how good Paris is in comparison to Romeo. She makes it sound as if Paris would be a much better husband, and it's the right thing for Juliet to marry him. The Nurse calls Romeo a 'dishclout', which is rude. On the other hand, she says Paris is 'an eagle', which makes him sound better than Romeo, and it's a simile. It is also an example of hyperbole. Juliet doesn't know whether to believe the Nurse because she was saying nice things about Romeo before, and now she's changed her mind.

It doesn't say why the Nurse has changed her mind and is no longer loyal to Juliet in the extract. It could be that she thinks it is too dangerous or a waste of time to wait for Romeo to come back. Or it could be that she is scared of Lord Capulet, who has just been shouting at Juliet. But she really believes what she says because in the extract she says that she speaks from the heart.

Juliet is not very happy with the Nurse's reaction and asks her if she really means it. 'Speak'st thou from the heart?' This is a question that means she can't believe the Nurse means it. She is upset because the Nurse has betrayed her, so loyalty is really important in the play.

Writing about loyalty and betrayal – try it yourself

Activity 9

You have identified some of the weaknesses in the student response in Activity 8. Now, use what you have learned to rewrite and improve the same essay.

> **How does Shakespeare convey the importance of loyalty in this extract from Act 3 Scene 5 and in the play as a whole?**

a. Look back at the extract in Activity 6 on page 85. Follow the three steps below to improve the student's response. Write your notes on separate paper.

   Stage 1 – Make notes and organise your ideas. Check the comments you have made on the student's response opposite and make sure you have included the following:

   • lacks opening argument with a main idea

   • references to language and structure do not comment on the effects

   • vocabulary is repetitive and not very precise or ambitious

   • lacks any reference to big ideas or context

   • no reference to Shakespeare in the response

   • no conclusion to answer the question set in the task.

   Stage 2 – Decide on the main argument for the introduction. Consider using the third statement in Activity 5 on page 84 to start your introduction:

   > Shakespeare condemns those in the play who fail in their loyalty, and he punishes those characters who betray others; he is completely in favour of loyalty.

   Stage 3 – Consider how to include language, **structure** and context. Use the notes you have made on the extract on page 85 to include comments in the essay on the effect of each of these methods:

   • Juliet's emotive use of language

   • the Nurse's use of **hyperbole** or exaggeration

   • Juliet's simple questioning of the Nurse

   • the structural choice of where this scene comes in the play.

b. On separate paper, write your improved response to the exam-style task. You should aim to write around 500 words.

Control and freedom

Key ideas about control and freedom

1. There are figures of authority in the play, such as Prince Escales, who control events and maintain social order.

2. The theme of control encompasses parental control, the law, religion, social and gender restrictions and even fate.

3. In *Romeo and Juliet*, Shakespeare presents characters who assert their freedom through resistance or rebellion, engaging the sympathy of the audience.

4. Fate, or fortune, is portrayed as a powerful force, dictating the future.

5. In the play's ending, Shakespeare seems to applaud the bid for freedom, but appreciates the return to order.

Key quotations

'A pair of star-cross'd lovers take their life' (The Chorus, Prologue)

'This day's black fate on more doth depend' (Romeo, Act 3 Scene 1)

The repeated 'd' sounds like a funeral bell, creating a sense of doom; the black **imagery** reinforcing the ominous hand of fate.

'If all else fail, myself have power to die' (Juliet, Act 3 Scene 5)

'then I defy you, stars!' (Romeo, Act 5 Scene 1)

Key events and structure

Act 1 Scene 1
Following the disorder in the opening scene, the Prince declares death as the punishment for further fighting.

Act 1 Scene 2
Lord Capulet arranges the marriage of his daughter to Paris.

Act 1 Scene 5
Lord Capulet forbids Tybalt from challenging Romeo at the ball.

Act 2 Scene 2
Romeo and Juliet defy their families to meet secretly.

Act 3 Scene 1
The Prince exiles Romeo as punishment for the death of Tybalt in a display of public authority.

Act 3 Scene 5
In an example of domestic authority, Lord and Lady Capulet insist Juliet marry Paris, but she refuses.

Act 5 Scene 1
Hearing of Juliet's death, Romeo defies the law and the 'stars', reinforcing the ever-present importance of fate and fortune.

Act 5 Scene 3
Romeo and Juliet kill themselves, but peace and order is restored.

Exploring control and freedom
Means of control

Shakespeare contrasts control and authority with freedom and independence. The control is shown in many different guises: the rule of law, social conventions, religious expectations and the authority of parents. Above all of these authorities is the presence of fate or fortune, predetermining people's lives entirely beyond their control.

a. Select three quotations from the relevant parts of the play that demonstrate the control or authority exerted by the following characters.

Lord Capulet	
The Prince	
Friar Lawrence	

b. Summarise the typical characteristics of those in the play who have control and authority over others. Think about their age, their social position, their gender, etc.

The bid for freedom

Audiences often view a bid for freedom as courageous and appreciate characters who are willing to sacrifice themselves. Romeo and Juliet are the main characters in the play who seek the freedom simply to love each other and defy the powers that control their lives.

a. Complete the table with examples of how and why each character defies different types of authority and control.

Juliet defies:	Explanation
her parents	
the family feud	
the decree of exile	Secretly meets Romeo for wedding night despite him being exiled
gender expectations	
Christian beliefs	
Friar Lawrence	

Romeo defies:	Explanation
the Capulet guards	Climbs the wall, avoiding the guards, to see Juliet on her balcony
the family feud	
the decree of exile	
the law	
Christian beliefs	

b. Summarise what you have learned about how Romeo and Juliet respond to authority.

Fate and fortune

In Shakespeare's time, many people believed in fate – a supernatural force determining events against which individuals have no control. In the play, characters also refer to fortune, which is a **synonym** for chance or luck, to show that things just happen, without any plan. This is mixed with references to the heavens, which usually indicates that God is controlling events. This is a powerful narrative device as it makes the characters, and the audience, feel that events are inevitable.

a. For each of the quotations below, identify who is speaking and what it tells us about their attitude to fate and fortune.

   i. 'O, I am fortune's fool.' (Act 3 Scene 1)

   ----

   ii. 'Alack, alack, that heaven should practise stratagems
   Upon so soft a subject as myself!' (Act 3 Scene 5)

   ----

   iii. 'If all else fail, myself have power to die.' (Act 3 Scene 5)

   ----

   iv. 'then I defy you, stars!' (Act 5 Scene 1)

   ----

   v.   'O here
   Will I set up my everlasting rest,
   And shake the yoke of inauspicious stars
   From this world-wearied flesh.' (Act 5 Scene 3)

   ----

b. Summarise what you have learned about the influence of fate and fortune on the events of the play.

Activity 4

Both Romeo and Juliet are subject to a range of different authorities and control over their lives. How they deal with the events that take place tells us about their sense of responsibility and resilience.

Of Romeo and Juliet, who is more likely to blame fate when bad things happen, and who is more likely to take decisive action? Explain your answer, and what it tells us about their characters, with examples from the play.

Interpretations of control and freedom

Activity 5

The themes of control and freedom are morally complex. Are all forms of control bad, and is all freedom good? Should the characters be free to make their own choices, regardless of the consequences for others? Shakespeare challenges the audience to consider how far control or freedom are necessary in society.

a. Read the following interpretations and decide which most closely fits with your ideas about the play. Circle your choice.

> By choosing to die, Romeo and Juliet bring about a more peaceful and harmonious society; their sacrifice was not in vain and it demonstrates Shakespeare's support for social change.

> Romeo and Juliet never stood a chance: Shakespeare shows that every type of authority and power was against them, even fate itself, suggesting a pessimistic view of society as unchangeable.

> Romeo and Juliet attempt to follow a difficult path, balancing freedom of choice with the restrictions of society, but it is fate, Shakespeare argues, over which they have no control, which finally does for them.

b. Explain your choice of interpretation, using examples from the play to support your view.

Writing about control and freedom – with support

Activity 6

Use these next activities to practise writing about the theme of control and freedom. Underline and annotate the key words or phrases in the following exam-style task. What precisely are you being asked to do?

> **How does Shakespeare present ideas about fate in this extract from Act 1 Scene 4 and in the play as a whole?**

Romeo	I fear too early, for my mind misgives Some consequence yet hanging in the stars Shall bitterly begin his fearful date ← With this night's revels, and expire the term Of a despised life clos'd in my breast, By some vile forfeit of untimely death. But He that hath the steerage of my course Direct my sail! On, lusty gentlemen. ←	personification of fate, linked to fear and bitterness mood shifts from gloomy to cheerful with exclamation mark

Tip

Where the extract is short, make detailed notes to comment on the language and any other structural or dramatic devices used. Try looking at every single word to see where there is useful material for your answer. Sample annotations have been made to the extract to help you.

Activity 7

a. Make notes on the extract to show how Shakespeare:

- conveys the idea of a supernatural power and its negative effects

- makes references to future events

- references God as a kindlier guide

- changes the **mood** from abstract and sinister to more physical and concrete.

b. Using these notes, summarise your response to the task in one sentence and use this as your main argument.

Activity 8

Read the following student's excellent response to the task in Activity 6 on page 93, along with the examiner's notes.

On separate paper, write a final comment as if you were the examiner commenting on what you think makes this an excellent response.

EXCELLENT

Romeo attempts to follow a difficult path, balancing freedom of choice with the restrictions of society, but it is fate, Shakespeare argues, which finally does for him. In this extract, Romeo recognises that he is in the hands of a powerful supernatural and evil force over which he has no control.

The extract comes as Romeo and his friends are going to the Capulets' party. The speech stands out as being a pause in the action. Romeo is still moping over Rosaline and hasn't met Juliet yet, so this is an important moment for him when he feels the fateful 'consequence' of 'this night's revels' might be something terrible. The personification of 'consequence' shows that he feels the presence of a higher power at work.

He says that his future is 'hanging in the stars', which creates an atmosphere of fear. The word 'hanging' has connotations of death, as well as suggesting that the future is held in the balance. It is as if he makes one wrong move and it will be too late – his fate will be sealed. This increases the sense of inevitability and tension for the audience, created by the Prologue at the start of the play with the image of the 'star-crossed lovers', suggesting they are doomed. The words 'bitterly', 'misgives' and 'fearful' indicate that the fate he faces is not a positive one, as they are all ominous and bode badly for Romeo.

Romeo calls his life 'despised', as if fate has targeted him specially. These negative thoughts are echoed in the final scene of the play when Romeo says that he has carried a 'yoke' of 'inauspicious stars' and his death is the ultimate end. It is almost as if Romeo has given in to bad luck. He speaks about paying a 'vile forfeit', as if Fate were playing a game with him. This feeling is shared in the play by Juliet who also feels as if she is being played with like a toy. But whereas Juliet takes decisive action and declares that if all else fails, 'myself have power to die', Romeo seems to have less resilience and gives himself up to his fate.

Romeo turns to God for guidance and asks him to 'Direct my sail.' This shows that Romeo is caught between the goodness of God and the evil of his fate. The final line brings Romeo, and the audience, back to real life as a reminder of the physical, everyday world rather than the supernatural undertones felt by Romeo. Shakespeare ends the play with that same life brought to a sudden end, as fate decreed. The message is clear: there is no way of cheating fate.

The student opens with a main argument: that Shakespeare shows how the power of fate was too great for Romeo. They bring in big ideas, such as society and freedom of choice.

The student comments on the position of the extract, making a point about structure and the impact on the pace of events. They also pick up on the language used to link back to the focus on 'fate'.

Detailed analysis of the language and imagery follows, with clear connections made between Shakespeare's word choices and his intentions.

The student offers deeper interpretations of Romeo's response to fate. They also make comparisons with Juliet and make a distinction between their reactions to fate, linking back to 'freedom of choice' from the introduction.

Writing about control and freedom – try it yourself

Use what you have learned to plan and write your response to this exam-style task.

> **How does Shakespeare present ideas about authority in this extract from Act 3 Scene 1 and in the play as whole?**

Prince	And for that offence
	Immediately we do exile him hence.
	I have an interest in your hearts' proceeding:
	My blood for your rude brawls doth lie a-bleeding;
	But I'll amerce you with so strong a fine
	That you shall all repent the loss of mine.
	I will be deaf to pleading and excuses,
	Nor tears nor prayers shall purchase out abuses:
	Therefore use none. Let Romeo hence in haste,
	Else, when he is found, that hour is his last.
	Bear hence this body, and attend our will:
	Mercy but murders, pardoning those that kill.

a. Add annotations on how the theme of authority is shown in the extract. You might find it helpful to consider the following questions.

   • What is Shakespeare's purpose in providing a voice of authority?

   • How important is order and control in this scene and in the play as a whole?

b. Summarise your response to the essay task in one sentence and use this as your main argument.

   ----

c. On separate paper, plan your answer. For each point you make, ensure there is an opportunity for you to comment on the language, structure or **stagecraft** Shakespeare uses to convey that point.

d. On separate paper, write your response to the task. You should aim to write around 500 words.

alliteration   the use of the same letter or sound at the beginning of adjacent or nearby words. For example, *pickled pepper*

antagonist   a person who is hostile to someone or something; an opponent

aside   words spoken so that only certain people, or the audience, will hear them

characteristic   a quality that forms part of a person's or thing's character

connotation   an idea or feeling that is suggested by a word in addition to its basic meaning. For example, 'red' carries the connotations of danger, stop, love, passion, blood and anger; 'green' carries connotations of the natural environment or feeling ill or jealous

context   the setting or circumstances in which something was written and the way in which it is presented

contrast   a difference seen when things are shown together

couplet   a pair of lines, typically rhyming and the same length (sometimes known as a rhyming couplet)

dialogue   the words spoken by characters

dramatic irony   a literary technique by which the full significance of a character's words or actions are clear to the audience, but unknown to the character

foreshadow   to be a sign of something that is to come

genre   a particular kind or style of literature or art

hyperbole   a dramatic exaggeration that is not meant to be taken literally. For example, *I've got a stack of work a mile high*

imagery   visually descriptive or figurative language used to convey an idea

imperative   a form of a verb used in making commands. For example, *Come in, come here!*

irony   a literary technique where the intended meaning differs from what is said or presented directly

juxtaposition   the placing of two or more things next to each other to show how they are different

metaphor   a form of words in which one object is described as if it really is another (rather than just being 'like' it); for example, *the news was a bombshell; her iron will was obvious in her face*

mood   the tone or atmosphere conveyed in a literary or artistic work

motif   a repeated design or theme

narrative   the telling of a connected sequence of events

personification   the use of human features, behaviours or characteristics to describe an animal or something that is inanimate

platonic love   love that is close and affectionate but not sexual

protagonist   the main character in a play

rhetorical question   a question asked for dramatic effect and not intended to get an answer

simile   a comparison between two things which asserts that one is 'like' the other. For example, *his eyes were as black as coal; the clouds were like wisps of cotton wool*

soliloquy   a speech in a play in which a person speaks their thoughts aloud when alone or without addressing anyone else

stagecraft   skill in writing or staging plays

symbolise   to represent something with a symbol, especially an object chosen to represent an abstract idea. For example, the sun could be said to represent life, hope or growth.

synonym   a word with a similar meaning to another word

tragedy   a serious play about the death or downfall of the main character

unrequited love   love that is not returned